HIGH
ADVENTURE

HIGH ADVENTURE

THE ADVENTURE DOESN'T END
WHEN YOU BECOME A DAD

MIKE ALLSOP

ALLEN&UNWIN

SYDNEY•MELBOURNE•AUCKLAND•LONDON

Allen & Unwin
Level 3, 228 Queen Street
Auckland 1010, New Zealand
Phone: (64 9) 377 3800
Email: info@allenandunwin.com
Web: www.allenandunwin.co.nz

83 Alexander Street
Crows Nest NSW 2065, Australia
Phone: (61 2) 8425 0100

A catalogue record for this book is available from
the National Library of New Zealand.

ISBN 978 1 76063 362 2

Design by Megan van Staden
Set in Excelsior and Calibre
Printed and bound in Australia by Griffin Press, part of Ovato

10 9 8 7 6 5 4 3 2

MIX
Paper from
responsible sources
FSC® C009448

The paper in this book is FSC® certified.
FSC® promotes environmentally responsible,
socially beneficial and economically viable
management of the world's forests.

To my mum, Joan, who taught me
there is no such word as can't

CONTENTS

INTRODUCTION

I am not going to lie. When I found out that Wendy was pregnant the first time, I really thought my life as an adventurer was going to be over. Back then, I thought I was living the dream—I was working as an airline pilot and climbing mountains in my spare time. I could go wherever I wanted and embark on whatever challenges took my fancy. I mean, it doesn't get better than that, right?

Wrong! Having kids has made our lives so much richer and so much more exciting—and, in many ways, it's been just the beginning of my life as an adventurer. I still get to do all the things I love doing, but now I get to do them with the people I love the most in the world. You've got to admit, that is pretty cool.

Now, that's not to say that it's always been easy. Wendy and I have put in the hard yards to find a way to make adventuring with the family work for us and for the kids. It's involved us having a lot of faith in each other and more than a little bit of courage. There's this thing I call momentary courage. It's the courage you have in the moment of time required to take the first step. The courage you have in that moment will change your life.

The great thing about having momentary courage is that it means you don't have to be brave all the time—just in the moments when it counts. I've had many such moments in my life, and I can look back now and see times when having that little bit of courage has changed the course of my life drastically.

When I was climbing Everest, I had this huge feeling of doubt just before we were due to head for the summit. There were a lot of 'what if?' stories rolling through my mind. But it only took courage for that one moment to decide to go for it and I was 100 per cent in!

In some ways, climbing Everest is like going adventuring with my kids—but with a completely different set of risks to navigate. The courage, commitment and determination required are the same when it comes to climbing Everest or taking the whole family to spend three weeks at altitude in a tiny Sherpa village.

When Wendy and I sit down and talk about possible family adventures, a whole lot of dreams and ideas fly around and I've got to say some of these ideas are way outside the box— and that's OK, because outside the box is often where the fun lives. Some of the ideas stick and some don't. Choosing what we're going to do is much like making any big decision in life, really.

We all know that feeling when you're at a bit of a crossroads and you have a choice about which direction to take. One direction might be safe and secure, while another brings with it a little niggle of doubt. Deep inside, you know that if you set off in that direction you might not make it all the way. It's at those times that you need momentary courage. Sometimes the most courageous thing to do is to recognise the risks and take the easier route, but sometimes you have to take that first step on the path that's lined with challenges. Then things just seem to roll and you start thinking outside the box and you find your momentum.

When I first took Ethan adventuring, he was seven and I was terrified. There we were, trekking in the Himalaya. Ethan was quite happy, while I was scared that I might not be getting the whole parenting thing right. Gradually, though, I began to see that he was loving it and that I was doing a good job.

One of the best things about taking the kids adventuring is seeing them learn about life outside of their comfort zone and seeing them recognise just how much they're capable of. What I've realised through our adventures together is that, once you achieve something that you didn't know was possible, you develop a whole new set of beliefs—and these beliefs allow you to go on to achieve even greater things.

Throughout all of my adventuring, there have been two things I've learned not to do. This first is never to listen to the naysayers. There will always be people who have opinions about how you choose to live your life and how you choose to parent your children—and you're not always going to agree with their opinions. If they're people who are significant to you, whose opinions you trust and who have your best interests at heart, then absolutely take their views into account. But if they're not any of those things then take no notice. Every adventure I've ever done—either on my own or with the family—has had its fair share of naysayers, of people who for whatever reason thought I was doing the wrong thing. If I stopped and listened to them, I would never have achieved anything in my life. Instead, take heed of those people who support you and who believe in you; they're the ones who really have your back.

The second thing I've learned not to do is fear failure. If you're afraid to fail, you'll be afraid to try. I truly believe that fear of failing has killed more dreams than actual failure ever has. The only true failure is never having tried. If you're thinking about taking your kids out adventuring or if you're looking for new ways to connect with and spend time with them, ask yourself this: what would you do if you knew you couldn't fail? Whatever those things are, going out and trying them is an awesome place to start.

I know that the type of adventures we have with our kids aren't going to appeal to everyone. When it comes to one-on-one adventures with our kids, I always make sure I listen to them when they talk about what they want to do and what it is they want to achieve. That way we're sure that we're all getting something out of what we're doing. It doesn't have to be something huge or epic—the reality is that kids just love spending quality time with their parents.

When it comes to planning an adventure, I've developed three super simple tools to help me get things done.

1. DRAW A (DEAD)LINE IN THE SAND

Put a time frame on your adventure—write down a start date and record what you're planning to do. This helps you to believe you are on your way and gives you something to work towards. It also tells your subconscious mind that something that was a dream is about to become a reality.

2. BASIC BRILLIANCE

If you do the basics well, then you're 90 per cent of the way there. When it comes to adventuring with kids, the fundamentals are safety, health and happiness. If both you and the kids are safe, healthy and happy throughout your journey, then you know you're doing well. If you ever begin to feel overwhelmed or if things feel a bit out of control, it's time to focus on the absolute basics and nothing else. Once you realise that you have the basics sorted, you'll find a little more capacity to cope and you'll get your momentum back.

3. MOMENTARY COURAGE

In that one moment, be courageous. Take the first step. Whatever it is that you want to achieve, whatever is important to you—whether it's committing to an adventure or committing to making the most of your life—then take that step and go out and conquer your mountains!

CHAPTER 1

AN ADVENTURER IS BORN

Growing up, I was a very quiet, shy boy. Truth be told, I probably held on to my mother's skirt too much. When I was eight, my parents split up, which made me even more timid and withdrawn. One of my early memories from that time is of Mum loading me and my brother, Bob, into the car while Dad stood there on the front steps of our house crying.

For the first couple of years, I saw my dad every second weekend. To be honest, I didn't really care how often I saw him. I just liked spending time with him, hanging out, fixing my bike, doing normal father–son stuff. We even trained up for a ten-kilometre fun run together, and I used to love going on training runs with him.

One of our next-door neighbours in Titirangi, Auckland,

where we lived, told me years later that he once saw Dad sitting outside our house, waiting, for ages. He'd come to see us, but Mum had taken us out. I'm not sure what arrangements Mum had made with Dad, or whether she knew he was going to be there.

When I was around ten, he stopped seeing us altogether. Mum had told him he had to see us regularly or not at all, and he chose the not-at-all option. I know Mum just wanted us to have some stability in our lives, but it was really sad that the two of them couldn't work out a visiting arrangement between them. Looking back, it was one of those situations where there were three sides to the story: Mum's side, Dad's side and the truth.

Mum did everything she could to make up for Dad not being around, but I still grew up thinking that I must have done something wrong for my father not to love me. I would cry at night because he wasn't there. Whenever I did something good, like getting a prize at school, the thing I wanted most was for my dad to see it or just to know about it—but he never did. His absence always took a little bit of the shine off the good things that happened to me.

I only saw Dad once after he left us. It took me 26 years to meet up with him again. He told me that it had just been too hard for him; that he thought it was better that Bob and I didn't have to see all the fights between him and Mum, even though that meant him not being in our lives. That made me really sad because I hadn't cared that he and Mum fought. I just wanted a dad.

Mum and Dad's split impacted more than our family life. It also meant that we had to move house. Mum worked really hard and kept Bob and me in a private school until the end of intermediate. Then I left my little private school—which had about 200 students in total and no more than 20 to a class—and was thrown into a huge high school with 1800 students. I felt completely lost and withdrew into myself even more. This, combined with my family situation, left me feeling

Looking back, it was one of those situations where there were three sides to the story: Mum's side, Dad's side and the truth.

deeply insecure. Suddenly nothing was as it used to be.

To make things worse, I was badly bullied when I was in my early teens. The main offender was a guy called Paul. He had an older brother who dealt weed and generally ran on the wrong side of the law. Eventually, someone informed on Paul's brother and he got busted by the police. For some reason, Paul decided that it was me who had talked to the cops. I'm not sure why, because I had no idea what either of them got up to.

One lunchtime, while I was playing tennis, Paul got ten of his friends together and they stole my schoolbag and took it behind a classroom. When I went to get it, the ten boys formed a circle around me. As I bent down to pick up my bag, Paul punched me in the face—twice.

I was a good few inches taller than him, so I stood up tall, raised my arms and shouted, 'What did you do that for?'

I was on the edge of fighting back and letting him have it—to this day I really wish I'd had the courage to do just that. But I didn't.

It didn't matter, though. Realising that I was bigger than him and I had a bit of fight in me, Paul rounded up his pack of cowards and walked off, leaving me very shaken.

I went home and told Mum what had happened. She hit the roof and straight away set off to Paul's house. I don't know what was said there, but she sorted it out and he never came near me again. Even so, that incident really shook the tiny amount of confidence I had in a big way. I withdrew socially even more. Deep down, I was very unhappy.

I can see now that there is a time and place for your mum to jump in and help fight your battles, and then there are times when you need to stand up for yourself. If I had fought back, in some ways I think I would have been better off, even if I had taken a beating.

As a result of that incident with Paul, I found it hard to focus and really started to struggle with my schoolwork, and I had a terrible year. It even affected my summer holidays, as I spent a lot of time worrying about the coming school year, which was going to be huge. I was going to have to sit my School Certificate exams. I knew these exams could determine my future and I was worried.

I felt this passion, this drive inside me to become a pilot. I went to bed thinking about it and woke up thinking about it.

Then a fleeting moment changed everything for me. One afternoon, I noticed a plane flying over our house in Titirangi. It was an Air New Zealand Boeing 747-200, and it looked huge as it slowly made its way to Auckland airport. As I watched, I started to imagine how it would feel to fly a plane like that for a job.

Just like that, my dream was set: I wanted to be a pilot.

Then I started thinking about all the things that could get in my way. I was shy, I'd had a terrible year at school and my marks weren't the best. That's when I remembered one of my mum's favourite sayings: 'There's no such word as can't!'

I felt this passion, this drive inside me to become a pilot. I went to bed thinking about it and woke up thinking about it. I decided I was going to do everything within my power to make that dream come true.

When I went back to school at the start of the year, I focused my full attention on my schoolwork. In order to help my studies, I asked one of the smartest kids in my maths class how long he was going to spend studying for one of our exams. He said he'd spend about 20 minutes. I thought that was great, and I went home and did exactly 20 minutes of study.

I sat the exam, confident that following the smart kid's study plan would get me across the line . . . and I failed. I got 46 per cent. The smart kid got 92 per cent. That made me really mad.

The following week, we had another exam. I wasn't about to risk the smart kid's study plan again, so I studied for four hours during the week. Exam time came around and I was nervous. Surely this time I'd pass.

Again, I was shocked when I got the results—but this time in a good way. I got 95 per cent and topped the class! That's when the penny dropped. I realised that brains had nothing to do with it. It was how hard I was prepared to work that was going to make the difference. I would just have to work harder than the next guy.

As well as working hard at school, I had two after-school jobs. I worked at the local supermarket two nights a week and all day on Saturday, and I also had a paper round one day a week. I earned a weekly total of $36. Unlike a lot of teenagers, I wasn't in a hurry to spend my wages. I was saving them for something special: flying lessons.

In a life-changing stroke of luck, Gary Spicer, who was an Air New Zealand pilot, heard that I wanted to learn to fly. I was friends with Gary's son, who must have told his dad about my dream to be a pilot. Gary struck a deal with me—if I rented the plane, he'd teach me to fly. An hour in a Cessna 152 cost $70, so I could afford one a fortnight. Gary's generous offer saved me the extra $15 an hour an instructor would have cost.

I taxied out, took off, flew a circuit and landed all on my own. I was 16 years old. The freedom of it was incredible.

I did my first lessons with Gary, then one of his friends took over for the final few sessions before I could fly solo. My new instructor was another Air New Zealand pilot, David Morgan. (David went on to become the airline's chief pilot.) He was an excellent teacher and he was always very honest with me when I made mistakes. One Saturday, his feedback consisted of: 'That was a shocking display of flying. You didn't trim the aircraft once and your checks were sloppy. I'm not wasting my time on a Saturday morning teaching you to fly if you're going to fly like that. We'll do another one and if it's no better I'm going home!'

After that next circuit, David got me to pull over, then smiled and told me I was ready to do my first solo flight. This was a huge deal for me, as it is for every pilot. I taxied out, took off, flew a circuit and landed all on my own. I was 16 years old. The freedom of it was incredible. Afterwards, I taxied over to collect David, who was standing on the tarmac watching me. He congratulated me and I couldn't have been happier.

Since I had grown up without a father, having people like Gary and David look after me throughout my flying training was significant. They really helped to shape me into the person I am now. These two men gave their time to help me fulfil my dream. I will always be grateful to them for that. They also taught me how important it is to put my time and energy into helping the young people around me. You really never do know when your actions might change a young person's life for the better.

As well as getting me closer to my goal of being a pilot, taking these lessons meant my self-confidence grew, as did my self-belief.

Once you achieve something you thought was impossible, you develop a whole new set of beliefs. It was these new beliefs that allowed me to go on and achieve the things I have in my life. It really doesn't matter if you are 16 years old or 66 years old. It all comes down to your belief in yourself.

CHAPTER 2

A FAMILY
OF FIVE!

With my new confident outlook, I continued towards my goal of becoming a commercial pilot. Here's where Jim Bergman comes in. Jim owned Great Barrier Airlines, and he would sometimes hire out their Britten-Norman Islander aircraft to young pilots who were looking to do some type-rating training (training on certain types of aircraft). Jim made me an offer I couldn't refuse: 'Five hours of flying you pay for and I'll give you another five of co-pilot time for free.' I was in awe, as Jim had quite a reputation as a great aviator. I couldn't quite believe I was going to be flying with him.

Not only did I fly with him, but I ended up flying for him. Once I'd done all the necessary training, Jim offered me a job working with him at Great Barrier Airlines. I spent four years with Jim and the team, flying between Auckland and the island, doing ferry flights from the United States and in the Pacific, and working as a pilot in Fiji.

There were adventures aplenty for a young pilot, and I learned a hell of a lot about life and flying, but the biggest adventure of my life started a few weeks before I left the airline for my dream job. Yep, I'd landed the big one: I was going to be a pilot for Air New Zealand. But first, I had to work out my notice at Great Barrier Airlines. Not long before I left, I headed to a 21st that was being held in a shearing shed on the island. That night, I was sitting on a hay bale when I saw this girl walk in. I can remember it so clearly—she had long dark curly hair, beautiful eyes and these stunning lips. She looked like a supermodel. Within a few minutes I was introduced to her—her name was Wendy—and we started chatting. Then we danced and spent the entire evening talking and laughing. We just clicked.

When it came time for her to leave the island and head home, Wendy was on my flight, but I failed to get her phone number. I wondered if I would ever see her again. Luckily for me, fate intervened when one of the other pilots came to see me with a jacket he'd found on the aircraft. It belonged to Wendy's sister. I found Wendy's phone number on their booking, called and asked if I could drop off the jacket.

While I was there I asked her to come over to the island with me and have lunch. She agreed, and we've pretty much been together ever since—even after I spewed on her boots at my farewell party on the island. Hilariously, Wendy told me a few years later that was the exact moment she fell in love with me!

▲

I absolutely loved working as an international pilot for Air New Zealand (and I still do!). My first few years were really exciting, as I got to explore new cities and meet heaps of new people, but it also meant I was away from home a lot. That was quite tough on my relationship with Wendy, but we always found ways to make it work.

The weirdest thing for me was suddenly not having a goal to work towards. I'd been so focused on becoming a pilot for so long, but now that I was one I no longer had something to aim for. After a couple of years of being away on long duties I began to feel a bit rudderless, but I couldn't quite work out what was wrong or how to change it. It was like I'd lost my mojo.

The weirdest thing for me was suddenly not having a goal to work towards. I'd been so focused on becoming a pilot for so long, but now that I was one I no longer had something to aim for.

I needed a new goal, so I plucked one out of thin air: I decided I'd run a marathon. But I couldn't seem to get inspired about it; I didn't even make it to the start line. I pulled another random goal out of the air: I would do the Coast to Coast multisport event in the South Island. I failed to see that through as well. It wasn't until I took a huge step back that I realised I'd failed because I wasn't passionate about either of those things. I decided to just relax, open my mind and dream. I read a heap of books and magazines about different adventurers. I read a lot of Ernest Hemingway's books, and absolutely loved *The Sun Also Rises*, which is about a bunch of people going to Pamplona in Spain for the running of the bulls. As a result, I decided that I was going to run with the bulls as well.

Wendy came to Spain with me and she was sitting in the arena as I came running in with all the bulls. It was an awesome adventure. It wasn't until I got back to New Zealand that I found out Hemingway hadn't run with the bulls; he'd just watched. Classic.

My dreams were focused around adventure and I started reading about climbing, in particular Mount Everest. But I thought it was impossible.

Then one night I was out for dinner with a friend in Los Angeles. Talk turned to what we wanted to do with our lives and my friend Herwin said he wanted to climb Mount Everest as well. It sounded ludicrous to me, but here was another of those life-changing moments. That night I dreamed about summiting Everest. A seed had been planted in my mind. My focus had returned. I had a goal: I would climb Mount Everest.

I didn't let the fact I had no climbing experience hold me back. Over the next few years, I spent as much time as I could in the mountains. The first of these was Tanzania's Mount Kilimanjaro—a mountain that would come to hold a special place in my life.

One of my reasons for heading to Africa instead of the South Island was Wendy. From the very start, she always backed me in whatever I wanted to do, including climbing. One of the reasons our relationship works is that she loves adventure just as much as I do, but not in the same way.

She has always been super supportive of what I do and enjoys being a big part of it, right down to the nitty gritty of planning. Her dreams and her adventures differ from mine—hers tend to involve a few more home comforts—but we respect each other as individuals and encourage each other to follow our dreams. Wendy likes her five-star holidays, while I'm more of a zero-star person, but the more I respected her five stars the more she respected my zero stars. That's where Africa came in. Wendy had always wanted to do the traditional Kiwi OE, travelling around the world and living overseas, but meeting me had put a spanner in the works and she'd never managed to go.

One of the reasons our relationship works is that Wendy loves adventure just as much as I do, but not in the same way.

I bought a house and Wendy moved in with me. We got two flatmates to help pay the mortgage. Julie and Nic were both nurses from Canada. It wasn't long before I realised that my best mate, Mat, had started hanging around a little more than usual. Long story short, he and Julie ended up getting married!

After a while, Wendy and I talked about her going on an OE on her own, and we decided that if she wanted to travel then she should go and live and work in London for a year. Being an international pilot meant that I could fly up every month and see her. The theory sounded good but when it came to putting the plan into practice, the separation strained our relationship. We decided we needed more than just a night here and there, so I booked six weeks' leave in which I climbed Mount Kilimanjaro and met Wendy in Greece for a holiday together.

All up, Wendy spent eight months living and working in London. I was happy that she was doing something she really wanted to do, but I was equally happy when she came home! I'd missed her terribly and had done as much climbing as I could to take my mind off it, including a summit of Mount Aspiring.

When Wendy returned from London, she walked straight back into a nursing job, so our combined salaries meant we could actually afford to buy a house together. It was in a nice area but it was a complete do-up. Pretty much everything had to be fixed but, hey, we love a challenge.

Now that we were in the same country and in our own home, there was quite a lot of pressure on us to tie the knot. Wendy and I were getting on well but I just didn't want to get married. Watching my parents split up when I was so young had really affected my view of marriage. I didn't think it was for me. At one wedding, I started playing a little drinking game with myself: every time someone asked me when I was going to marry Wendy I would have a drink. A bit of a dumb idea! Let's just say, I eventually lost count and I don't remember much of the wedding.

While everyone else was hassling me about marrying Wendy, the one person who didn't seem to be worried about it was Wendy. She could see that my past had a lot to do with my hesitancy and she was happy with things the way they were.

One weekend, I was tidying the section at our house while Wendy had gone to a travel agent to book a holiday to Thailand with some friends. When she got there she was feeling sick so she came home. I don't know why, but I asked her if she was pregnant. She laughed and reckoned it was impossible as she was on the pill. But I wanted to be sure so I went down the road and bought a pregnancy test. Even though Wendy was convinced she wasn't pregnant, she agreed to take the test just to shut me up. I waited outside the bathroom and it took a long time—a really long time. Much longer than the time it takes to pee on a stick. Finally, I knocked on the door and went into the bathroom. Wendy was just sitting on the bath staring at these two little blue lines. 'I'm pregnant!'

Pregnant? Are you f-ing kidding?

I was stunned. Our lives were about to change in a huge way.

Over the next few months, I spent a lot of time trying to come to terms with the fact that I was going to be a dad. I was all over the place and couldn't really understand what was going on with Wendy.

I spent a lot of time trying to come to terms with the fact that I was going to be a dad. I was all over the place and couldn't really understand what was going on with Wendy.

When Wendy got pregnant, she changed and it wasn't good. At first I thought she'd turned into a total cow. Like a lot of guys, there were times when I thought my life was over, that I was stuck if I married Wendy. I didn't want to get married.

One day, just before I was flying to Sydney for work, we had an argument about nothing really. I went off to work thinking, 'How can I possibly marry this woman?'

Thankfully, a friend had given me a book called *Every Guy's Guide as to What to Expect When She's Expecting*. I had it with me in Sydney and I decided to give it a read. I sat in a park and read the book from cover to cover. It all made sense—perfect sense. This book laid it all out for me. Wendy wasn't a cow; she was just awesome, amazing. It was me who was being a dick. Wendy was just experiencing normal pregnancy hormones. That day I decided I would marry her, but I wasn't going to be rushed or pressured by anyone or anything. I would ask her when the time was right.

I had thought Wendy would want to change me now that she was pregnant, but my fears were completely unfounded. She knew who I was, she knew what drove me and how much I loved mountaineering and adventure. Despite her pregnancy and everything that was going on in our lives, Wendy supported my climbing and refused to entertain the thought of me cancelling a trip I had planned to Russia. And it went both ways: I was happy to support Wendy to keep doing the things that mattered to her. So, Wendy stayed home and prepared for the arrival of our baby while I flew to Russia to climb Mount Elbrus—the highest peak in Europe. I'd already climbed Africa's highest mountain, so why not?

Mount Elbrus is in a bit of a tricky place. Situated in the Caucasus Mountains, it sits right on the border of Russia and Georgia. It's also quite close to Chechnya, where the fight for independence from Russia has been long and bloody. To say the region is dangerous is a bit of an understatement.

Reaching the 5642-metre summit after an epic effort, I didn't feel as elated as I'd expected to. As I staggered up and proudly stood on the summit of Europe, I started to cry. They were not tears of joy, though—I was feeling homesick. I was such a long way from home and I was alone. Wendy was at home pregnant with our first child, and here I was on top of a mountain with a thunderstorm about to roll in. I knew I wanted to keep climbing, but I also knew that I would need to change a few things so that my new family would always be a part of it.

On my return to Auckland, my entire focus was on Wendy and preparing for the birth of our first child. When our son, Ethan, finally arrived it was just magic. The emotion I felt was indescribable. I was so happy to be a dad, and I was sure I was the proudest dad in the world.

Wendy was a totally natural mum and I couldn't have been happier with our little family. But I had absolutely no idea about how to be a father and I was nervous about getting it wrong. Thankfully, when I went looking for help I found a company called Parents Inc, which is now known as the Parenting Place. They taught parenting skills and I learned a lot from them about how to be a good dad.

One of the most vital lessons I learned was that kids spell love T-I-M-E. Time spent with kids is what they value above all else. It's that simple. Parents Inc also talked about the importance of starting family traditions, which give kids something to look forward to and to look back on when they are older. These ideas were to come into play for me as my kids got older.

Meanwhile, Wendy and I both adjusted to having three of us in the house, and I continued working my butt off to make sure that house was as perfect as it could be for the two most important people in my life.

It was fantastic to be a new dad, but I was a little worried that I wouldn't be able to spend as much time in the mountains as before. I thought Wendy wouldn't want me going climbing any more, and I also thought that I'd want to spend so much time with the baby that I might lose my drive to climb. Thankfully, Wendy knew how important adventuring was to me and she had no intention of trying to change me. I like to think that no one can change anyone else, but that we all need to change and evolve to make life as good as it can be.

A few months later, with our new little family completely thriving and the house looking pretty good as well, I set off on another adventure. This time my mission was to climb New Zealand's highest mountain, Aoraki Mount Cook.

Before I left, Wendy and I went to our lawyers and I filled out a form giving her full power of attorney. I also made sure that I had a decent life insurance policy so that Wendy and Ethan would be provided for if anything happened to me. With every climb comes risk, but I knew I was climbing with one of the best and most experienced guides in the region. Confident that nothing much would go wrong, I promised Wendy that I would be off the mountain in nine days' time to meet her and Ethan for a family holiday in Wanaka.

So it was that I climbed Aoraki Mount Cook with two other climbers. That nine-day thing I told Wendy about very nearly didn't happen though. One of our guides described the forecast as 'a little stink' for the next few days, but he didn't think it would be too bad. Yeah, right.

En route to the summit, across the Hooker Glacier, there were gusts that reached about 80 knots and were impossible to stand up in. Then I fell into a crevasse, which my fellow climbers pulled me out of. After that, we ended up crawling on our bellies the last 30 metres to our hut on account of the huge winds. That was when we found out that the hut door had frozen solid and we spent an hour cutting the ice away from the doorframe so we could get in! Little did we know that we'd be stuck at the hut for a couple of days . . .

On the third day, the weather settled and we decided to carry on up the mountain. We made it up to Empress Hut, nearly running some of the way as we were concerned about possible avalanches after the recent bad weather. On the way up, the cloud rolled through the valley below us and I could hear the roar of avalanches lower down the mountain.

Thankfully, the avalanches stayed away from us and I eventually made it to the summit of Aoraki Mount Cook. Standing at the top of New Zealand's highest mountain fuelled my dream. Everest felt even closer to becoming a reality for me.

We found out that the hut door had frozen solid and we spent an hour cutting the ice away from the doorframe so we could get in!

When we got back to Wanaka, Wendy was there to meet me. She ran over and gave me a huge hug. Then she pulled away just a little and I stared into her eyes, expecting her to say something romantic. But no. The next words out of her mouth were, 'Poo! You stink!'

Back at the hotel, she ran a bath and insisted I sit in the tub and scrub myself with some industrial soap and a wire brush until the smell had gone!

I sat back on the sun lounger at the hotel while Wendy got me a beer and dressed my wounded feet. Then she said, 'Close your eyes. I have something to show you.'

My heart stopped.

'You're not pregnant are you?'

'Just close your eyes, OK?'

With that I felt her drop a wad of paper into my lap. When I opened my eyes I saw it was a property contract. Wendy had bloody bought a house! She had used the power of attorney that I signed over before I went into the mountains. I couldn't believe it.

We had put in a tender for this house a few months earlier, but had been unsuccessful. We decided that it wasn't meant to be, and I had completely forgotten about it. But obviously Wendy hadn't. She's just as determined as I am when she puts her mind to something!

▲

I decided that the perfect time to ask Wendy to marry me was just before I left for a climbing trip to Peru. I was planning to climb 5947-metre high Alpamayo in the Peruvian Andes, then have a crack at nearby Huascarán, which at 6768 metres would make ideal training for Everest. I would be climbing with Wanaka guide David Hiddleston, who had summited Everest a few years before.

On the night before my departure, Wendy and I went to her parents' house to drop off eight-month-old Ethan for the night. While I was there I pulled Wendy's dad aside and asked for his daughter's hand in marriage. Tears welled up in Brian's eyes and he was a bit speechless but he agreed.

Having got Brian's OK, I took Wendy out to our favourite Japanese restaurant. While we were eating our starters the conversation somehow got on to marriage. Wendy said with a tear in her eye, 'You're never going to marry me . . .'

At that precise moment, the lights dimmed with just one spotlight left on over our table. Wendy looked a bit confused. Then a waiter brought out our dinner platter. Among the many beautiful dishes on it, sitting on top of a rose, was a diamond ring. The spotlight caught it and it sparkled like a star. Well, a small—no, make that tiny—star!

Wendy's eyes lit up and a huge smile came across her face. She turned to me and I said, 'Babe, will you marry me?' She burst into tears and gave me a hug.

'So is that yes?' I asked.

'Yes, yes, yes,' she said.

The next day, Wendy and Ethan waved me off at the airport. Wendy had the wedding to plan while I was away and I felt good. I knew I had made the right decision, and was happy that I hadn't rushed it.

The Alpamayo climb was a very technical climb. From the summit, the view across the Peruvian Andes all bathed in glorious sunshine was something else. The sense of achievement I felt as I looked across it was indescribable.

Then it was on to Huascarán—a mountain that eludes me to this day. On the way up to base camp, I had been coughing a little and not feeling a hundred per cent, but I hoped I would shake it off. Unfortunately, after a few hours I started feeling much worse. Eventually, I collapsed into base camp coughing and wheezing, unable to even speak. I lay on the ground and slept for a few hours.

That night was very rough, and I was feeling really sick. The next morning I decided to head back down the mountain. I was feeling a little better but didn't want to back myself into a corner at high altitude. If the weather changed while we were at a higher camp and I got any sicker, I could very easily die.

While I was waiting in nearby Huaraz, I heard there had been a big accident on Alpamayo. A huge cornice had collapsed off the summit and gone flying down the route we had just climbed, killing eight climbers. Without a doubt they were the climbers we had camped next to and spent time with at base camp on Alpamayo.

It didn't really sink in. The closest way I could describe it is it was like hearing someone you had met had been killed in a car crash. I felt very sorry for them and for their family, friends and loved ones. But it seemed somehow removed. Sure, I had been climbing the exact same route and mountain a few days ago, but I didn't really think about getting killed myself.

Truth be told, I was more worried about how my family would take the news in relation to my mountain climbing. I knew how dangerous it was, but this would be a bit close for them. I called Wendy straight away. She seemed OK, a little worried. I guess she simply put it out of her mind and accepted that mountaineering and adventure was part of the man she was going to marry.

▲

Over the next few months Wendy was busy planning our wedding. I was just happy to be getting married, so I generally nodded my head in agreement. For me it wasn't so much about the actual ceremony.

Before the wedding, Wendy and I met up with my guide David Hiddleston and his partner, Anna, for dinner. Wendy and David got on instantly and chatted away. Before long the conversation turned to Everest. Wendy asked David about a climber called Rob Hall.

Rob was an expedition leader during the May 1996 disaster on Everest when nine people were killed on the mountain, including Rob himself. Rob had tried to help a sick client down during a storm and had become trapped at the south summit of Everest. His client, Doug Hansen, died. Hall had managed to stay alive for a few nights but no one could help him. While he was stuck there, he managed to radio through to base camp and was patched through to his wife back in New Zealand. During that radio call they named their unborn child. Most of base camp was listening to the heart-breaking conversation. Rob died a short time later.

Wendy didn't hold back when she was talking to David. She was very straight up about what she thought of Everest and risking your life on the mountain, especially when young children were involved. I sat back and stayed out of the conversation, as it was Wendy's time to talk to someone who had actually been on Everest and lost friends there.

It was very hard to listen to her fears and worries, but at the same time I could see her understanding more about what drives someone to want to summit Everest.

After dinner we said goodbye to David and Anna. David wanted to meet Ethan so we met up the next morning for coffee. That was to be the last time I would see my friend, as he and Paul Scaife were killed in an avalanche on Mount Tasman late in 2003.

▲

Before I knew it, it was our wedding day. I stood next to my best man, Mat, my buddy Brendon (aka Pinky) and my brother, Bob. When Wendy appeared, my heart almost stopped. She looked so stunning, all dressed in white with her beautiful dark hair flowing down her back. Tears welled up in my eyes, and I started to feel a little dizzy. Wendy and I stared into each other's eyes and exchanged our vows. I remember thinking about the life we would have together. It had sure been lots of fun so far.

The next afternoon, Wendy and I left for Rarotonga on our honeymoon, leaving Ethan with Wendy's mum. We had a fantastic time and talked a lot about our plans for the future. I really wanted another baby, but Wendy wanted to wait a little bit. I got my way in the end as it was on our honeymoon that our little girl, Maya, was conceived. It was quite a turnaround that I was the one who really wanted to have a baby and not Wendy.

Wendy realised she was pregnant again a few weeks later, and this time I knew what to expect. This pregnancy ended up being a little more difficult than the first one for Wendy, and Maya was overdue. On Friday, the doctor said that if she hadn't arrived by Monday Wendy would have to be induced. That night we got an extra-hot curry from the local Indian restaurant, hoping that a spicy meal might move things along.

Wendy woke at 4am with a really sore tummy.

'You're in labour,' I said.

Wendy reckoned she wasn't as the feelings were completely different from last time.

After a few minutes it was very obvious she was having contractions. Huge, random contractions. They were four minutes apart, then 30 seconds, then three minutes. We were completely unprepared for a home birth.

I called Wendy's sister Penny, who arrived very quickly. Thank goodness, as Maya showed up not long after she did.

I shouted to Penny, 'Quick! Get some boiling water and towels.' I don't know why that would be even remotely useful but I had clearly been watching too much TV. Unfazed, Penny ran off to do what I'd asked.

I dialled 111 and, just as the operator answered, Wendy let out a bloodcurdling scream. I could hear the operator shouting, 'What's going on?'

I looked down and what I saw made me drop the phone. Maya was face up, eyes closed, with the umbilical cord wrapped around her neck. Her face was completely blue. Out of nothing but instinct I grabbed the cord and pulled it clear of her neck. There was no gentleness. She had to come out right now.

Maya was face up, eyes closed, with the umbilical cord wrapped around her neck. Her face was completely blue. Out of nothing but instinct I grabbed the cord and pulled it clear of her neck.

'OK, Wendy, the head is out. Big push on the next contraction.' The contraction started in a few seconds and I pulled Maya out. Wendy slumped forward and passed out semi-conscious on the bed.

I now had the most precious little baby in my hands, but she wasn't breathing and she was blue. It was a true moment of life and death that could have gone either way. After clearing the baby's tiny mouth, I turned her over onto her tummy. She was still not breathing, but just as I leaned forward to begin to give mouth-to-mouth she let out this huge cry. My heart filled with total joy.

After a few days of being looked after at Birthcare, Maya was pronounced healthy and we were able to take our very precious cargo back home. Wendy was a fantastic mum and life was a whole lot busier with a newborn and a 22-month-old.

Climbing took a back seat for a while, and it was actually Wendy who encouraged me to go climbing again. I think she knew what made me happy and she didn't want a grumpy husband moping around. My next goal was to head to Nepal and climb Ama Dablam with legendary Everest guide Henry Todd. He was a bit fussy about who he would take up Everest so I booked an expedition with him to climb Ama Dablam in October 2005. I had a year to do some hard-out training and equally hard-out saving.

In the meantime, normal life went on. I had been promoted to first officer on a Boeing 767 and was now flying all over the Pacific Rim. This was great as it allowed me lots of time overseas to buy climbing gear and it meant that Wendy, who was now a full-time stay-at-home mum, could come away with me on work trips, bringing one of the kids at a time. Wendy and I talked a lot about a third child and decided the time was right to try.

One morning, Wendy walked into the kitchen and said, 'I have a surprise for you.' She handed me a pregnancy test with two lines on it. I knew full well what it meant, but it didn't compute. There was less than a week to go before I left for Nepal to climb Ama Dablam, which at 6812 metres was the hardest mountain for me yet.

I must have looked a bit stunned and spluttered, 'Does this mean I can still go the Nepal?'

Wendy gave me a look that didn't even need words. 'You mean that's wonderful news. And, yes, you can still go to the Himalaya.'

'Oops, sorry . . . aaahhh . . . I mean, that's fantastic. Sorry, babe!'

The night before I was to depart, I had a very bad moment. For some reason I was really scared. I wasn't sure that I should be going climbing in the Himalaya with a young family at home. I tossed and turned all night and couldn't sleep.

The next morning, I talked to Wendy about how I was feeling. She simply said, 'You have to go. If you don't, you'll regret it for the rest of your life. We'll be fine here, Mike. This is something you know you have to do.'

Wendy dropped me at the airport and I said goodbye to her, Ethan and Maya with a tear in my eye. This was my biggest adventure yet but I was going to miss them terribly.

▲

Arriving in Kathmandu for the first time is something no one could forget. What a place! I was in sensory overload. There were hundreds of people going about their business, sacred cows wandering along in the middle of the road, dogs, goats and lots of monkeys everywhere, and tons of motorbikes zipping in and out of traffic.

I had arranged the whole climbing trip through Henry Todd and I was to meet him at Ama Dablam base camp. I trekked there with another group who were going to be climbing Ama Dablam out of the same camp.

We spent the first night in a tiny village called Monjo, and the next day we tackled our first challenge: the hill up to Namche Bazaar. Here we went from 2500 metres to over 3350 metres, with most of the altitude gained over a steeply winding track.

We spent a couple of nights in Namche before heading off on the 13-hour trek to Pangboche, which would become my favourite village in the Himalaya. It is the last village that is inhabited all year round on the way to Everest. Most of the Sherpa on Everest come from Pangboche and, sadly, when you start talking to the local people you realise the toll that Everest and altitude have had on this tiny community. Everyone has lost a close family member to either Everest, Ama Dablam or altitude sickness, as Pangboche is about 4200 metres high and most of its inhabitants work in the climbing industry.

We arrived in Pangboche, then had to walk another 20 minutes up the hill to Upper Pangboche, where we would be staying with the local lama. His name was Lama Geshe and he was the head teaching lama for the entire area. He had escaped Tibet during the Chinese invasion in the 1950s along with the Dalai Lama. It was such a privilege to be staying in his home.

The next morning I woke early, went down to the tea room and found a seat. Lama Geshe came in and gestured what I thought was 'good morning'. He spoke Tibetan and Sherpa (very similar languages). Next thing, his son came into the room and said to me, 'Sir, you are sitting in the lama's chair.'

I was horrified. I jumped up and moved away apologetically, but Lama Geshe wanted me to sit next to him. We ate breakfast together and, even though neither of us could understand a thing the other was saying, we had a very interesting conversation.

That night, Lama Geshe noticed a book I was reading called *My Quest for the Yeti* by Reinhold Messner. The first man to climb Everest without oxygen, Messner was also the first person to climb all 14 peaks above 8000 metres—and all without oxygen. But this book wasn't about his climbing. While in the Himalaya, Messner said he'd had an encounter with an animal that stood up on its back legs right in front of him, then circled around behind his back. He also says a similar creature had chased him for miles. These sightings sparked Messner's 20-year hunt to find out what the animal was—an undiscovered bear or the famous yeti?

Their son relayed the discussion to me. 'Father is saying the yeti attacked Mum's friend at the back door five years ago and Mum is saying, "NO! It was nine years ago!"'

Lama Geshe pointed to my book and, through his son, I asked if he had ever seen a yeti around Pangboche. Next thing, Lama Geshe and his wife got into a heated discussion. Well, actually she got heated; Lama Geshe just laughed.

Their son relayed the discussion to me. 'Father is saying the yeti attacked Mum's friend at the back door five years ago and Mum is saying, "NO! It was nine years ago!"'

While the yeti is a creature of folklore in the West, it seemed to be a very real threat to the people of Pangboche. One thing was for sure: I wasn't going walking at night on my own around this village.

Later that evening, I heard the tale of the famous

Pangboche yeti hand and skull, which had been stolen from the monastery in the 1950s. The person who stole it not only took precious artefacts from the village, but also robbed the monastery of its small income from people who would pay a few dollars to look at the yeti remains.

The next morning, our little unofficial team—me, Henry and the other climbers—sat down and were given a formal blessing by Lama Geshe. He chanted mantras and told us we were now blessed and would have a safe journey, but I noticed he didn't say it would be successful. He must have seen so many climbers who didn't make the summit of whichever mountain they were climbing, and probably plenty who never made it home.

His blessing did the trick for me, though, and I managed to summit Ama Dablam as planned despite other climbers along the way assuring me that it was harder to climb than Everest. No pressure, guys! When I got to the top, I could see Everest. It looked so close, towering above us by 2000 metres. I knew that I was looking at my ultimate goal.

On our way back down the mountain, I decided to go and see Lama Geshe again as we passed through Pangboche. I knew he didn't usually see people he didn't know, but I thought I would try anyway.

I knocked gently on his door and his daughter, Tashi, answered. She went and asked if he would see me and he agreed. I entered his tea room and bowed down low before him. He welcomed me with a huge smile. It's hard to describe but I felt this sense of calm on seeing him. We spoke for a little bit, with Tashi translating. I told him that Wendy was expecting our third child. There was a bit of discussion and Tashi said, 'My father would like to name your unborn child.'

I must have looked a bit shocked as the next thing Tashi said was, 'Father says you don't have to if you don't want to.'

'No, no! I am honoured, but my wife doesn't know you.'

'Father says, "Go home and tell your wife I have named your unborn child, but do not tell her the name. Once the child is born the first question she will ask is 'What's his name?' and she will agree to the name."'

Lama Geshe started chanting a mantra, then he stopped and spoke to Tashi. 'His name will be Dalha. His name means one who is great, like you.' At that point, we didn't even know the sex of the baby but somehow Lama Geshe did.

While we were talking, I asked him if he was worried about the world. He said, 'Yes, I'm worried as there seems to be many bad people.' He then spoke about the importance of giving to others. 'If everyone just gave a little more than they took, the world would be a better place.'

Those words have stuck with me and I do my best to live by them.

▲

Wendy, Ethan and Maya picked me up from the airport. It was so good to see them. Ethan was now three and a half and Maya was 15 months old. They had all grown in the month I had been away. Wendy looked just beautiful. She had this glow about her and a tiny little bump showing.

After I had arrived home and unpacked my bags, with the help of two little toddlers clambering through my climbing gear in search of presents, it was time to tell Wendy about the name Lama Geshe had given our unborn child.

I explained the story and that I had a name but I couldn't tell her what it was until the baby was born. She didn't look that impressed, but at least she didn't say no.

Over the next few months, life returned to normal. I was still flying the Boeing 767 around the Pacific Rim and my longest trip away was only a week. This was a lot better for my family than when I was flying long haul. Even so it wasn't easy leaving them for that length of time on a regular basis. But it was the price Wendy and I willingly paid so that I could do a job I loved.

It wasn't easy leaving them for that length of time on a regular basis. But it was the price I willingly paid to be doing a job that I loved.

With Wendy's due date approaching, we went to see the midwife. There was some discussion about being at home for part of the labour, as we had planned to be for Maya's birth. I couldn't believe it. The trauma of Maya's birth was still vivid in my mind. I could see this tiny little baby—my daughter—lying limp in my hands, blue and not breathing. It was too much for me and I burst into tears. Both Wendy and the midwife got the shock of their lives as they were happily chatting away.

'I can't do it. I just can't! There is no way I can handle you being in labour at home. I'm sorry. I just can risk going through that again. The first sign of labour, I want us to go to hospital,' I gulped while tears streamed down my face. The plan was quickly changed.

Our son was born in hospital without incident after a short labour. Thank bloody goodness. After his arrival, Wendy's first question to me was, 'Is he OK?'

I told her he was fine.

As Lama Geshe predicted, Wendy's second question was, 'What is his name?'

'Dalha,' I replied.

And so it was that Dylan Michael Dalha Allsop came into the world.

Over the next few months we settled into our busy life as a family with three young kids, but my Everest trip was coming around fast. I had planned to make my attempt in April 2007, but with Dylan's birth I had started to wonder whether it was a good idea.

Wendy and I sat down and talked about me climbing Everest. I told her I was happy to put it off for ten years, and that I didn't need to go now when the family was so young.

'No, I want you to go now when the kids are young. They won't remember you gone.'

I was shocked to get such a blunt response. 'You mean dead?' I asked, feeling a bit confused.

Wendy laughed. 'No! Gone for three months, silly. They're so young that they won't remember you being gone for three months. But when they're 12, 14 and 16 years old, their dad leaving the country for three months will be a huge deal. I want you to go now.' She never ceases to amaze me.

So it was on. I would be climbing Everest . . . Wow!

▲

For the next few months, I was so busy thinking about what I needed to do that I forgot to consider the impact my climb might be having on the people around me. That was until my little brother, Bobby, came to see me one day. The minute

I opened the door I could tell something was wrong. Tears welled up in his eyes and he looked straight at me and said, 'You can't climb Everest. I don't want you to do it. Please don't do it. I don't want you to die.'

We spoke for a bit and I tried to explain how I was mitigating the risks and doing things as correctly as I could, but I guess it doesn't make sense to anyone who doesn't climb. Eventually, he accepted that I wasn't going to change my mind. We hugged and I fought back tears.

Being away from my family for three months was one thing, but being away from work for three months was quite another. I couldn't afford to take leave without pay, so I had to get permission from Air New Zealand to take leave in advance. I wrote to my boss and explained that I had been accepted on an Everest expedition, and that I had all the finance and experience I needed—now I just needed the time off.

I was so busy thinking about what I needed to do that I forgot to consider the impact my climb might be having on the people around me.

Air New Zealand were amazing. I got a letter in reply fully supporting me, saying I could take all the leave I needed and simply pay it back over the coming years. I felt so lucky to be working for such a great company.

I then asked the company's public relations department for permission to wear the company's logo, a stylised koru, on my climbing suit. I felt that it would represent all my friends and colleagues from Air New Zealand who had supported and encouraged me over the years.

When it arrived, it was a perfect five-centimetre-square koru. I held it in my hand with a real sense of pride—I would be taking this to the summit of the world soon.

The night before I departed I wrote a letter to my best mate, Mat. It contained very clear instructions about what I wanted done in the event of my death. If I died high up on Everest I didn't want anyone risking their life trying to bring my body down. I simply wanted to be left on the side of the mountain; the mountain could take me. I also wrote my wishes for my funeral or remembrance service. It was one of the hardest things I've ever had to do. Even harder was handing it to Mat the next day. I told him not to open it unless he had to, so he understood what was in it. I knew I could count on him to carry out my wishes—we've been best friends since we were kids.

As the time came for me to clear customs and head for my flight, I hugged everyone, then kissed my three beautiful children and my wife. Wendy held me tight, tears welling up in her eyes. We said goodbye and I turned and walked off. I got only a few metres before I had to turn around and hug her again, tears streaming down both of our faces. I put both my hands on her cheeks and whispered, 'Don't worry, I'll be fine.' Then I turned and left.

After security, there is a public viewing platform above the concourse. I looked up and there were Wendy and the kids waving goodbye. It was so hard to walk away from them, but this was such a pivotal moment in my life. I waved one last time, then took a few deep breaths and walked to the departure gate.

While I was sitting waiting to board the flight, something clicked in my head. It was time to focus on Everest. I had to stop thinking about anything else. I spent the next two flights focused on two things: the summit, and coming home alive.

When I got to Nepal, I couldn't wait to see Lama Geshe. I can't really explain why. I just felt a sense of peace when I thought of him. I guess deep down I was very scared about what lay ahead for me, and the uncertainty over whether I would live or die, whether I would make the summit or not, weighed on me. The only thing that was certain was that the next few weeks would be some of the most defining of my life.

As I walked up to Lama Geshe's home, I could feel the emotion welling up inside me. There he was sitting at his table, a huge smile on his face. I walked over and bowed down, offering the lama my folded white khata—a silk scarf that is given as a mark of respect. He placed it around my neck, said a short prayer and touched his forehead to mine, then welcomed me to sit down next to him.

His daughter, Tashi, translated for me as I told Lama Geshe that my son now had the name Dalha. He smiled and laughed as Tashi spoke to him in Tibetan. He then started a mantra for our safety on the mountain.

Hearing the deep tone of Lama Geshe's chant was one of the most moving experiences of my life. Once again the tears streamed down my face; I couldn't stop them. His prayer lasted five minutes and when it finished I wiped my eyes and a sense of relief came over me. I was now safe, blessed. I felt that I could do what I had come to do.

In the week leading up to my turn to climb Everest, I spent a lot of time at the monastery in upper Pangboche. I would sit quietly in the corner of the courtyard with my eyes closed, imagining being on the summit, trying to conjure the feeling of standing on the roof of the world. Then I would imagine myself back safely at base camp.

A friend of mine at Air New Zealand had taught me another useful technique, which involved visualising the obstacles that I might encounter. I would picture the worst-case scenarios: getting caught in an avalanche, finding dead bodies, losing a climbing partner or getting seriously injured myself. I would let myself imagine this to the point where it felt almost real. Then, once I got to that stage, I would picture myself dealing calmly with everything that was thrown at me. It was a way of training my subconscious mind to believe that I had already coped with the event. If I did get lost in a white-out, for example, it would feel as though I had already dealt with it in some way. It's an incredibly powerful technique with all sorts of different applications, and I still use it today.

After plenty of acclimatisation time spent at the requisite camps along the way, I found myself at camp three, awaiting my turn to finally head for the summit. To be brutally honest, I was scared—really scared. I didn't know whether I would live or die. I was going to the summit, and I would meet my fate whatever that might be.

Before I left, my mother had written me a letter, but not just any letter. It was a very emotional letter. I re-read it while I waited. She wrote about how I was destined to be on Everest and that I had to go forward and follow my destiny. In the letter she included my birth tag, which she had kept for 37 years, and asked me to leave it at the summit of Everest. I also planned to release locks of hair from each of my three children, Wendy and myself from the summit.

Almost six long weeks after leaving base camp I was at the foot of the Hillary Step—a 12-metre wall of rock, snow and ice that is the last obstacle before the summit. I handed my camera to Lakpa Sherpa, who was with me, and asked him to take some photos of me climbing the step.

I strained my neck back and looked up. I could see rock on the left and snow and ice on the right. I clipped in and swung my axe high. It stuck well and there was a large foothold from all the other climbers before me. I moved on to the step. I looked down between my legs and the view below was just unbelievable—there was nothing but air beneath my feet. I didn't look down again until I was at the top of the Hillary Step.

At the top of the step, I climbed around a large rock and up a very steep bit back onto the ridge. From there it was an easy walk to the summit. I could feel the excitement building. I was going to make it.

I slumped into the snow, managing to turn around so I faced straight out towards Nepal. The Himalaya lay before me. I thought, *This is what happens to people when they disappear. I'm going to disappear.*

I should have known better than to be so cocky. No sooner had I formed that thought than a strange feeling came over me. Something didn't feel quite right. I started to feel disorientated and then I began staggering. I'd take one step then I would stagger again. My left leg collapsed, then my right leg collapsed. I slumped into the snow, managing to turn around so I faced straight out towards Nepal. The Himalaya lay before me. I thought, *This is what happens to people when they disappear. I'm going to disappear.*

Lakpa Sherpa followed me up a few minutes later, and he knew exactly what had happened: I had run out of oxygen. He reached into my pack and changed my oxygen bottle. I took a deep breath, then I had instant clarity. If it wasn't for Lakpa, I would still be sitting there today. It was a great view, but . . .

I got up and walked around a big rock to find my friend Dr Rob Casserley standing there with his mask pulled down. Rob and I had met on Everest in 2007. Now he was here, smiling at me. 'Mate, well done. You've done it!' He reached into his pocket and handed me his sat phone. 'Here you go, buddy. Call Wendy from the top.'

I still had a wee way to go, so we said goodbye and I slowly carried on up. There it was—the summit of Everest. I was a little shocked. A flood of emotion came over me and a voice came into my head, saying, 'You've worked so hard for this, Mike. You deserve it!' A tear rolled down my cheek under my goggles.

Then it was like someone had flicked a switch. This was no place for emotion—it was too dangerous. If you cry on Everest your eyeball will freeze. I was there to do a job. I turned to Lakpa and shouted, 'Four photos and one phone call!'

He looked surprised, because I'd told him I was going to be very quick, but he nodded and gave me the thumbs up. There was no one else around. Everest has a short summiting window—there are only 10–14 days per year when the weather is amenable to climbers—so it's very unusual to have the summit to yourself. I was a lucky man.

I took the final few steps and stood on the roof of the world at 8.45am on 24 March 2007—a day and a moment that changed my life forever.

Wendy had been waiting to hear from me all morning. It must have been terrible for her. She had gone to bed the night before knowing I was climbing high on Everest. I found out later that she had managed to wait until midday before she poured herself a wine and sat for a while on her own.

I sounded really bad, slurring my words, with the wind roaring in the background— not the romantic vision she had of talking to someone on the summit of Everest.

I found a spot just below the summit, pulled out Dr Rob's sat phone and dialled my home number. Then I realised I still had my hat, goggles and mask on. I put the phone down on my lap while I took off my hat, thinking, *If I lose this hat, I'm going to lose my ears.* I tucked my hat carefully under my arm inside my jacket. Next, I took off my goggles. Same thing: *If I lose these, I'll be snow-blind in a few minutes.*

As I pulled my oxygen mask down, with the outside air at –55°C and a wind of 25 knots, the condensation on my face instantly froze. It was excruciatingly painful. I clawed at the ice with my hands to try to wipe it away.

All this time, the phone line had been open and everyone at home was waiting with baited breath, listening to nothing but a huge, rushing wind noise. Finally organised, I picked up the phone and shouted over the sound of the gusts. 'Wendy, can you hear me?'

Wendy yelled back, 'Yes! Yes! I can hear you. Where are you?'

'I'm on the summit. It's really Wendy, windy.' (I got my windys and Wendys mixed up.)

Wendy said later that I sounded really bad, slurring my words, with the wind roaring in the background—not the romantic vision she had of talking to someone on the summit of Everest.

'It's really windy. I've got to go,' I hollered.

'Are you safe?' Wendy asked.

'Yes, yes!' I said.

'OK, go down now, Mike. Go down now.'

'I'll call you from South Col. Bye, I love you.' I didn't wait for a response before ending the call. It was really difficult to speak in that temperature and wind.

Apparently, back in Auckland, Mat refused to celebrate until he knew I was down safe. Wendy's oldest sister, who is always up for a celebration, wasn't having a bar of it and popped the champagne!

I put all my gear back on and sat on the summit again, pulling out the hair clippings from Wendy, Ethan, Maya and Dylan. I opened the small bag and released my beautiful family's hair from the roof of the world. Then I took out the birth tag that Mum had sent me and tied it to a snow stake just below the summit. This was a special moment for me.

I called Wendy again later from base camp. It was so good to hear her voice. 'Mike, you are such a bloody legend!' she said, and that was when I realised just how massive this achievement was. I'd never really thought about it that way. I couldn't wait to see her and I knew it wouldn't be long. She was leaving Auckland for Kathmandu that night to bring me home.

After a night in Namche, I walked to Lukla then flew to Kathmandu the following morning. Wendy was due to arrive on the same day. I checked into our hotel and I realised my last two showers had been a while ago—one in April and one in May. Total. I was quite proud of that, but I was pretty sure Wendy wouldn't be so thrilled. I went and bought some soap, shampoo and shaving cream. Then it was back to the hotel for a good scrub and a long sit on a Western-style toilet before going out to the airport to meet Wendy. I was hoping she wouldn't say 'Poo! You stink!' this time.

The airport was the same as ever—hustle and bustle everywhere. I saw Wendy coming through customs, and she looked so beautiful. I hadn't seen her for two months. We kissed and hugged like there was no one else around, much to the amusement of the Nepalese.

We hopped in a cab and battled our way through the city traffic to our hotel. Wendy was so excited, and it was very cool to have her with me on that part of the adventure. I had lost 13 kilograms on Everest and was really weak, both physically and emotionally, so having her beside me made me feel so much better.

Wendy looked at me and said one of the smartest things anyone has ever said to me. 'If you need to climb Everest again, don't worry. We will find a way.'

Being able to show Wendy the places I loved in Kathmandu made me realise something pretty important. Up until then, I had thought that if I bought her some jewellery after each climb it would somehow make up for me having been away. So there were the Alpamayo diamond earrings, the Ama Dablam diamond ring . . . You get the picture. While we explored Nepal together, though, I realised just what a stupid idea the jewellery had been. Those material things aren't what life is about; it was actually having experiences together that mattered most to both of us. Memories are the only thing we can take with us when we leave this world. I made a mental note of this and decided to work harder on it in future.

As we talked through the details of my climb, Wendy didn't so much as blink when I excitedly told her about a loose job offer I'd had from Dr Rob to do some guiding on Everest with him. I wouldn't be paid, but all the climbing fees would be covered. Wendy looked at me and said one of the smartest things anyone has ever said to me. 'If you need to climb Everest again, don't worry. We will find a way.'

I knew that she meant it, but what she said gave me the space to work out that my kids—aged four, two and nine months—needed a dad more than I needed to climb Everest again. And later, when I took a step back, I realised that the thing that made Everest so special wasn't the summit; it was the relationships I formed with my climbing friends and the Sherpa people.

Wendy and I took a few days to explore Kathmandu before heading to Pokhara in western Nepal, where we spent a night by the lake, watching the water buffalo from our candlelit dinner table. It was a world away from camping out on the slopes of Everest.

Finally, it was time for Wendy and me to head home. As we took off, I felt a little sad to be leaving Nepal. It is such a magical place.

I wondered if I would ever be back.

CHAPTER 3

WHAT NEXT?

After I got back home, it took a bit for me to adjust to life post-Everest. Going from climbing the world's highest mountain back to my day job and doing normal stuff like getting the groceries was quite a challenge. It probably took about a year before we all fully recovered from Everest. It took a bit of a toll on my relationship with Wendy. She'd had to hold things together while I was away and now I was home we had to work our way back to so-called normal life. Thankfully, with a bit of hard work and time, we came out the other side stronger than ever before.

I'm happy to admit I learned a few things throughout the whole process. One was to stop focusing on what my partner was doing, and to start looking at what I was doing. I learned to forget about anything Wendy did that bugged me and instead address my own mistakes and issues.

Life resumed its normal patterns. I loved my work, I loved being a dad and I loved spending time with Wendy. My focus had changed from personal adventuring to involving Wendy and all the kids in everything . . . There had to be something in it for everyone.

Slowly, things settled down enough for me to start thinking about another adventure, but my focus had completely changed. I had loved my ten years of climbing adventures and I look back on them with a warm heart, but I didn't miss them.

I couldn't see myself going climbing again until the kids had grown up, and that sat well with me. Every time I questioned myself, I would briefly think about the mess I would leave behind.

My family is so important to me that mountaineering seemed like an unnecessary risk. In fact, I couldn't see myself going climbing again until the kids had grown up, and that sat well with me. Every time I questioned myself, I would briefly think about the mess I would leave behind. For the rest of my kids' lives, my death would take its toll. I felt this responsibility not to take any more massive risks.

It was also important that I wouldn't be away for months on end. I'm lucky that Ethan is the only one who has any memory of me being away climbing. He reckons he can sort of remember the fuss at our house on Everest summit day. The other two were so young that they can't remember Dad being gone for long periods of time, and I don't want them to start now.

Wendy and I have a little tradition where we go to our favourite Japanese restaurant, Taiko, every six months or so. We sit at the same spot at the bar each time, we eat and drink way too much, and we talk about our goals, dreams and ideas for the future.

One of these evenings at Taiko, Wendy said that if I wasn't going to climb Everest again I needed to do something to fill my emotional tank. She suggested I could take people trekking to Everest base camp, and employ my Sherpa friends, and just be in the mountains, seeing Everest . . . Before I knew it, I was planning a recce to the Himalaya . . . with a twist.

At the same time, we were going to start a new family tradition: our son Ethan, by then seven years old, would come with me to see Everest—and when our other two children turned seven they would do the same. This tradition created the perfect opportunity for me to spend time with the kids, while also having an adventure, creating memories and doing something that I loved. We hoped it would be something the kids would enjoy, too, even if it pushed them outside of their comfort zones.

▲

So the planning began. I talked to Ethan's teachers and they agreed the trip would be an amazing experience for him and gave us their blessing. It was a bit of a big call to be taking a seven-year-old to a Third World country, let alone trekking at altitude in the Himalaya.

I was super excited about planning Ethan's trip and got him involved as much as I could. He loved coming with me to buy gear for him, and we did some mini treks up Mount Eden for practice. Ethan asked lots and lots of questions. 'Dad, in Nepal, what do we eat?' 'Dad, where will we sleep when we're away from home?' 'How high will we climb up Mount Everest?'

The trip with Ethan gave me a chance to suss out the details of my new little business trekking to Everest base camp. I wanted to do things a little differently from most of the standard trek companies — all of our Sherpa guides would be Everest summiteers and we would stay only in small family-run tea houses.

Sue Todd, who summited Everest a few years before me and runs her own trekking business, helped me lots with starting my own. She told me exactly how she worked her treks, talked me through the logistics and, importantly, introduced me to Iswari Paudel to help with my new venture. I had met Iswari a few times when I was climbing Everest, and he is the main man in Nepal when it comes to climbing Everest, getting permits and advice about trekking. He owns Himalayan Guides, a large company that does treks, adventures and specialises in Everest expeditions. Both Iswari and Sue were really generous with their time and advice when it came to my fledgling business, and their support helped me realise I could actually make a go of this guiding thing.

But first I would take Ethan on his adventure. Given I'd be exposing him to altitude and to Third-World health issues, I went to see Dr Marc Shaw, who runs Worldwise, one of the world's best travel medicine clinics. He gave me some good advice, but it would mean about seven vaccinations for Ethan. I explained to him that it was all part of the adventure and he understood. He had the shots in two sessions and he was so brave and didn't even cry.

Ethan was doing taekwondo twice a week and was naturally fit. We did a few more training walks near where we lived, and a few walks around the block with a backpack with a two-litre bottle of water in it. We would be going very slowly when we got to the mountains, so we would have plenty of time to acclimatise properly.

During these training walks, we talked a lot about all sorts of things. I think this is where our bond really started to develop. It's hard to explain, but our relationship felt different. I was still the dad, but somehow we connected on a new level. Sometimes we talked and talked, and other times we didn't talk for ages yet still felt connected.

I didn't have a very big budget for the trip, so I decided we'd fly stand-by, which airline staff get as one of their perks, to Hong Kong and then get a cheap flight to Kathmandu. The cheapest and best flight connection was with a budget airline from Hong Kong to Kathmandu via Delhi. It departed three hours after we were supposed to arrive in Hong Kong, which was perfect timing. Only it didn't quite work out that way—the flight to Delhi got cancelled, leaving us with a 13-hour stopover in Hong Kong. Still, I can think of worse airports to be stuck in, so that was OK.

While I had all the gear I needed for the trip, I'd decided to wait until we got to Kathmandu to buy some of Ethan's gear, as it's so cheap there. As we packed our bags together, I could see the excitement building in him. With each new piece of gear, he'd ask, 'What is this for, Dad? When do we use this?' Most of all, though, he was interested in what he'd be carrying in his own trekking pack, which would only be his rain gear and nothing else.

Maya and Dylan decided they'd help us pack as well.

Maya, who was five, knew that one day it would be her turn, and she had plenty of questions. I lost count of how many times I heard her say, 'When it's my turn, Dad' followed by a question. Our new family tradition was well on the way to becoming established.

On departure day, both Ethan and Maya had a taekwondo grading before Ethan and I flew out to Hong Kong. I worked that morning and turned up just as the grading was finished. Ethan had been jumping up the gym steps as part of his warm-up and had missed one, smashing his face on the wooden step and knocking out his two front teeth. There was blood everywhere. After a quick clean-up, he surprised everyone by continuing his grading and gaining a 100 per cent pass.

When I looked at Ethan's teeth and gums, they were bad. His teeth had pushed up and punctured his cheeks and tongue. He was upset, as he thought we wouldn't be able to go to Nepal that night. To be honest, his teeth looked so bad that I thought the same.

I took him to an emergency dentist who said that the teeth that had been knocked out were his baby teeth, so we would be fine to travel. What a relief!

Both Wendy and I were a little worried and decided to take the rest of the evening to decide if we should go or not. In the end, Ethan was fine and was raring to go, even with a sore mouth.

The whole family headed out to the airport to drop us off. As we said goodbye, Wendy whispered to me, 'Now, you be careful, OK?'

She knew my approach to risk—or, rather, risk management. I would always be thinking and looking a few steps ahead, and if my gut told me something wasn't right I would follow my instincts. In saying all that, she was pretty amazing to trust me taking our seven-year-old firstborn to the Himalaya.

I told him that there were two main rules: the first was that he had to look people in the eye when they were speaking to him, and the second was that he had to speak in a loud voice so people could hear him.

Ethan was buzzing on the flight and he had heaps of questions. One thing we talked about quite a bit were the rules for the trip. I told him that there were two main rules: the first was that he had to look people in the eye when they were speaking to him, and the second was that he had to speak in a loud voice so people could hear him.

To get him used to doing these things, Ethan started on the plane. If he wanted anything, he would have to ask for it himself. I also explained to him that the flight attendants work really hard, so if he needed to speak to them he would have to go to the galley instead of just ringing the bell.

As first, he was nervous, but once he'd done it the first time he was off, full of confidence.

During our lengthy stopover in Hong Kong, I decided to go and find out why our original connecting flight to Delhi had been cancelled. I was suspicious about the way the budget airline had handled our booking, because we'd been rebooked on a later flight almost instantly.

'That 9am flight hasn't gone for years,' I was told. They were still selling seats on a non-existent flight and then rebooking people to suit themselves! I guess it's true that you get what you pay for.

The later flight left at 10pm. We'd paid for two seats in a row of four, but when we got onboard a woman had stretched out over the whole row. I smiled and pointed, indicating that these were our seats. The woman's husband told us she had a sore leg and ignored us. I got a flight attendant to help and the woman reluctantly moved her feet.

Ethan and I sat down in a rush, as the staff were closing the doors. Ethan ended up sitting next to the man, and everything was fine until after take-off. But then, the man lifted Ethan's arm rest so that his wife in the far seat could put her legs over his lap and her bare feet on Ethan. He froze and looked at me in horror, as her feet were a bit smelly. I wasn't having that! I swapped places with Ethan and told the man that this was our seat, our space.

We had dinner, then Ethan and I both fell asleep. I woke a few times to find a pair of smelly bare feet on my lap! The first time I politely tapped the lady's feet and asked her to move, but by the third time I just pushed them off, which, hilariously, caused great offence. Thank goodness it was only a six-hour flight . . .

We had a night in Delhi before our flight to Kathmandu, so I'd booked us a cheap room near the airport. We got into the taxi and drove for about ten minutes. Ethan pointed out of the window at a sign, and said, 'There's our hotel!'

Behind the sign was just a huge pile of rubble. I panicked, thinking I'd had another internet-booking disaster.

Thankfully, the actual hotel was just around the corner. I'm not sure how many stars it was, but when we checked in the lift wasn't working and only half of the lights seemed to go. It definitely wasn't Wendy's kind of place!

Ethan woke up pretty early the next morning and was bouncing off the walls, eager to go for a walk. We left the hotel for a short walk and it was an eye-opener—we were deep in the heart of working-class Delhi. There were thousands of people going about their everyday lives. There was some really cool street food that I would have tried if Ethan hadn't been there, but I knew that if I bought it he would have wanted some as well and I didn't want to risk him getting sick this early in the trip.

If you're not accustomed to the local food you have to be a bit careful eating in that part of the world, including Nepal. I've only ever had food poisoning there once and it wasn't very nice. The statistics are pretty clear—66 per cent of all visitors to Nepal will get some sort of tummy bug—so I'm really careful, especially with the kids. One of the best things is to get them taking regular multivitamins, fish oil and probiotics for about a month before the trip in order to build up their immune systems. It can be a bit hard to make sure they take all their supplements, but I always tell them that it's way better to take pills than to be sick!

We found a little shop and bought some food for breakfast before heading back to the hotel. Everyone was very friendly and a few people said hello to us as we walked past. Then I noticed that the traffic was starting to build as everyone made their way to work. Next thing, a motorbike appeared at speed on the footpath straight in front of us. We jumped out of the way. Soon, every motorbike started using the footpath as a motorbike lane, up and down driveways, around lamp posts, dodging pedestrians. Ethan loved this and took it all in his stride as if it was perfectly normal. I was very glad when we got back to the hotel intact in time to check out and head back to the airport.

Once there, security was really tight. There were the normal checks, then another round at the gate and then an extremely rigorous check at the remote gate, right at the bottom of the steps to the aircraft. Ethan and I got chosen for the extra check and we watched as they searched every single inch of our bags.

Soon enough, we were airborne for the quick flight to Kathmandu. In the distance, I could see thunderstorms, but I didn't think too much about them until the captain came over the intercom and said we would be entering a holding pattern near Kathmandu airport until the storms had passed.

Every time we did a lap of the holding pattern, I could see in the direction of the airport and it wasn't looking very good. We went around and around in the sky for about two hours before the captain finally decided to divert to Lucknow, about 30 minutes' away, where we'd refuel before heading back to Delhi. Tired and hungry, we landed in Delhi almost 12 hours after we'd left. It wasn't the greatest start to Ethan's first visit to the Himalaya.

Customs had no idea how to process us as we'd arrived from India after departing from India! Thankfully, a senior customs agent appeared and ordered that we be cleared straight away. Then we were led to a bus that took us to the hotel where the airline was putting us up for the night.

As soon as we sat down, Ethan promptly fell asleep. He then slept for the whole 90 minutes that it took us to get to the hotel. When we arrived, there were spectacularly dressed traditional Indian guards to welcome us.

Ethan woke up just as we pulled up in front of the hotel. As soon as the bus stopped, the pushing and shoving started, as everyone piled off, rushing to reception to get a room. I soon realised that there was going to be no way this hotel had 150 spare rooms.

I spent the next 20 minutes explaining the term 'white lie' to a seven year old—not easy!

The reception staff were shouting, 'There are no single rooms—three people to a room!' I told Ethan to go back to sleep, or at least pretend to be asleep. I picked him up and walked into the lobby with him in my arms. A hotel manager rushed over, asking if he was sick. I said, 'He's just woken up. I think he could be . . .'

My tiny white lie paid off when the manager took us to a private room and got Ethan an orange juice. He asked if there was anything else he could get us. Quick as a flash, I said, 'A room would be great . . . before they all go.'

He came back a few minutes later and gave us a key. He peered at Ethan and said, 'He is looking a lot better . . .'

'It must have been the orange juice,' I said. 'Thank you for helping us.'

Ethan and I went to our room and I spent the next 20 minutes explaining the term 'white lie' to a seven year old—not easy!

The next morning, after breakfast and photos with the Indian guards, we boarded the bus and went back to the airport. Once there, we grabbed our luggage and went to enter the international terminal. An armed guard asked to see our tickets.

I handed them over and he looked and said, 'Sorry, not allowed in. These tickets are for yesterday.'

I explained that yesterday's diversion was the reason for the incorrect date, but he wasn't having it. 'No correct date, no entry. You go to Jet Airways office and get new ticket.'

Given head office was a four-hour return trip away in traffic and the flight left in two hours, I realised I only had one chance at getting into the terminal.

Making sure Ethan couldn't see, I turned my back and pulled out US$10 and folded it into the same ticket, then I politely asked the guard if he could please recheck the tickets.

'These are fine. You may enter,' he said, as he pocketed the cash.

At the gate, we went through all the same rigorous security again and boarded the flight. This time everything went smoothly and in no time we landed in Kathmandu.

CHAPTER 4

EVEREST WITH ETHAN

When you arrive in Kathmandu for the first time, it's all a bit overwhelming. There are hundreds of people everywhere, some asking to help with your luggage. Over the years, I've learned a little trick—I make sure I have a couple of US dollars in my pocket and I accept the help of the first person who offers to carry my luggage. Once you've given someone the job, everyone else leaves you alone.

We were met by a rep from Himalayan Guides who drove us into town, but not before welcoming us with some beautiful flower chains that he put around our necks. On the 25-minute drive to our hotel, I enjoyed watching Ethan take in all the people and the colour—his eyes were just about popping out of his head as he watched thousands of people going about their work, cars and motorbikes zooming in every direction in ordered chaos, not to mention the cows wandering in the middle of the road on account of being sacred animals in the Hindu religion. Ethan was like, 'Dad, look! A cow in the middle of the road! Dad, look! A monkey!'

When Ethan opened one of the windows, there was a big monkey just sitting there, looking at us.

We were staying at my favourite Nepalese-run accommodation, Hotel Manaslu. There, our room was decorated with traditional Nepalese art and wood carvings. When Ethan opened one of the windows, there was a big monkey just sitting there, looking at us. Ethan could barely believe his eyes—up until then, he'd only ever seen monkeys in the zoo. I wasn't so keen on our new friend, as it was almost as if he was saying, 'I'm just hanging out here, waiting for you to open the window, so I can come in and steal your stuff!'

I think Ethan got a bit sick of me being super careful, especially when I wouldn't let him swim in the hotel's beautifully tiled pool. I was so paranoid about him getting sick that I didn't want to take any chances. Needless to say, my approach has changed a bit over the years!

I did, however, loosen the reins a little the following day when we went off to Thamel, Kathmandu's tourist centre, to do some shopping. I got a good jacket and some walking poles for Ethan—both of which would be useful for the adventure ahead. There is so much hiking stuff available in Kathmandu that I reckon you could turn up there with US$300 and completely kit yourself out for a trek . . . except for underpants. There seems to be no underpants for sale in the tourist part of Kathmandu. Very strange.

When it comes to travelling with kids, jetlag is often an issue. I decided to apply the same tricks airline pilots use with time zones, and I did my best to get Ethan on the local time zone as soon as I could. That meant going to bed and getting up at local time, and trying to stay awake as long as possible until we'd adjusted. It was pretty easy to keep Ethan awake as he was so absorbed by everything that was going on around him.

That evening we had dinner in Thamel and caught a cycle rickshaw back to the hotel. Ethan thought that was just so exciting, and the look on his face made my heart melt.

The next morning, we were ready to leave the hotel at 6am to get out to the domestic airport. It's almost eerie on the roads at that time of the morning as there is no one much about—you can almost feel the city waking up.

Kathmandu's domestic airport seems chaotic, but it works. They know who is supposed to be on which flight, what luggage they have and exactly what the weather is doing in the mountains.

While we waited for our flight, a man asked me how old my son was. I couldn't see his face as he had a wide-brimmed hat on. 'He's seven,' I said.

'Wow!' the man said. 'That's cool. I came here when I was young like him. My father brought me here as well.'

Then he looked up at me. It was Peter Hillary, Sir Ed's son.

I was star-struck. I stuttered a bit, then blurted out, 'Peter, wow! Nice to meet you. I . . . I have tremendous respect for you. I've read about your climbing . . . Wow . . . I climbed Everest as well. Oh, this is Ethan. He's seven.'

It was so embarrassing. I felt like a complete dick, but it was pretty cool meeting Peter there given he'd first visited the country with his mountain-climbing father, and here I was bringing my son to see the Himalaya for the first time.

We chatted for a while, but Ethan turned a bit shy and didn't say much. As we got on the plane, Ethan said to me, 'Oh, Dad! That was *so* cool meeting Peter Hillary.'

While Ethan couldn't wait for the plane to take off, my mind had turned a bit to worrying. I knew that Wendy's biggest concern about this whole trip was the 30-minute flight we were about to take from Kathmandu to Lukla, which sits at almost 2000 metres above sea level. This is one of those flights that being a pilot makes a little bit worse, because I know too much.

The runway at Lukla is only 400 metres long and has a 16-degree upward slope with a 6000-metre mountain at the end of the runway, which means there is absolutely no option to go around once you commence the approach. Additionally, you're flying in the Himalaya, so the weather can change in a heartbeat. Every time I'm a passenger on this flight, I take my hat off to the pilots who manage to do it every day. There are only a couple of crashes at Lukla every ten years or so, but there are thousands of flights in and out of there every year. I knew the odds were low that anything would happen to Ethan to me, but that didn't stop me worrying.

While the flight is always a bit scary, this time it was much scarier because I had Ethan with me. I did my best not to let on to him that I was nervous. I just smiled and chatted about our plans for the next few days, all the while thinking, 'Is this worth it? Should I be doing this?'

As usual, though, the local pilots did an outstanding job and we landed safely. As soon as I could, I called Wendy to let her know we'd arrived safely. Not long after I first started climbing, we made an agreement that I wouldn't give her a detailed itinerary of where I'd be and when, and this continued into my trips away with the kids. Especially when it comes to flights, Wendy says she'd rather not know; that way she doesn't worry the whole time we're in the air.

Once on the ground in Lukla, we made the short walk over to Paradise Lodge. The owner, whose name is Dawa, was thrilled to meet Ethan and she made a real fuss of him. While we waited for our luggage to arrive, we ordered a big breakfast of fried eggs on toast, with a hot chocolate for Ethan and a Sherpa tea for me. Sherpa tea is a sweet milk tea made with yak butter, which might sound weird to a Kiwi, but it sure tastes nice.

As we were eating, Ethan suddenly sat bolt upright. Peter Hillary had just walked into the lodge and he was coming over to speak to us.

'How are you two guys going?' he asked, before turning to Ethan and saying, 'Wow! That's a scary flight, isn't it?' Then, he sat down and ordered some tea.

As we talked, Ethan pulled on my sleeve and whispered in my ear to ask if he could get a photo with Peter. I asked Peter, and he couldn't have been kinder. He and Ethan stood next to each other and posed for a few photos. Ethan couldn't stop smiling afterwards; he was absolutely rapt.

After a good catch-up over breakfast with Dawa, Ethan

and I were finally off on our trek. The first day is a long one, but it's over fairly flat terrain at about 2500 metres, which helps your body to slowly get used to the altitude—slowly being the key word there.

We had a great day with many stops along the way. It took me a while to work out that, if Ethan went ahead and stopped when he wanted to, we would cover much more ground. The key was keeping it fun. This was easy because there was always something different to look at—yak trains coming past, friendly locals who don't see many Western kids stopping to say hello or Namaste to Ethan, and of course the beautiful scenery . . . but no mountains yet.

All this time, Ethan was amazing. He just kept on walking without a lot of moaning or complaining. I think his attitude came down to both of our expectations aligning. Ethan knew that being on a trek means that you trek.

That first night we stayed in a little tea house at a village called Phakding. It was warm in the dining room, but absolutely freezing in the rooms. My little temperature gauge said it was 3°C. Out came the Icebreaker thermals for us to sleep in, and I explained to Ethan the importance of keeping his hat on as 30 per cent of body heat is lost through the head. He thought it was pretty funny to sleep wearing a hat but he soon got used to it. I also deployed a little trick that my friend Lakpa Thundu Sherpa had taught me years before on Ama Dablam. I filled my Nalgene drink bottle up with hot water and put it down inside Ethan's sleeping bag. These bottles are designed to last in cold and hot conditions and are a great piece of kit.

The next morning, we both woke early as we were still on New Zealand time. Making the most of the early start, we had a good breakfast and set off towards Monjo, which was an easy three or four hours' walk away. Most trekkers do a single long day from Lukla to Monjo, but I decided to split it in two and just take it slowly to help Ethan acclimatise.

As we walked along, I didn't feel any pressure to talk or keep Ethan entertained—although we got into the habit of going through maths times tables over and over as a way to pass time, which was slightly odd but kind of cool. Somehow, I felt like there was an unspoken bond growing between us.

At that point, everything sped up. The yak came running down the track, straight towards me and Ethan.

As we approached Monjo, we met two young Sherpa boys who were bringing their yak down from the village. The yak was misbehaving and wouldn't do a thing the boys asked of it. This huge beast stopped about 30 metres in front of Ethan and me. Then, almost in slow motion, one of the boys raised a big stick high into the air, and cracked it down hard onto the animal's back.

At that point, everything sped up. The yak came running down the track, straight towards me and Ethan. We ran to the left towards the edge of the track and the yak did the same. It was only a few metres away from us and it was moving fast. We then darted right . . . and so did the yak. A split second before it hit us, I grabbed Ethan by the scruff of his neck and threw him off the track and into a bush, then jumped in after him. The yak thundered past with the Sherpa kids running after it. We were safe. We climbed out of the bush and back onto the track, then looked at each other and laughed nervously. 'Err, let's not tell Mum about that, eh, buddy?'

We spent that night at Monjo and headed off the following morning for the big day: the dreaded Namche hill. It's just under six kilometres between Monjo and Namche Bazaar at the top of the hill, but the altitude change is about 800 metres—from 2600 metres to 3400 metres. The first few hours are relatively easy, then it's straight up on a path that has heaps of switchbacks, back and forward, back and forward.

This is where we first started feeling the altitude. Ethan and I were both huffing and puffing, and taking big rests every 15 minutes or so. As we sat resting on a rock, I looked at my altimeter watch and saw that we were now above 10,000 feet (3040 metres). Back home, it is a requirement to be on oxygen when flying above 10,000 feet in light, unpressurised aircraft, but here I was trekking at the same altitude with my seven-year-old son and it didn't seem to worry him in the slightest!

As we trekked, heaps of porters passed us. They each carried loads of around 35 kilograms, but some would carry double loads for double the money. They were paid 500 Nepalese rupees per load—the equivalent of about NZ$6.50. Most had really bad shoes or plastic sandals. They all had straps around their heads, which helped to support the baskets they were carrying, most of which were loaded to twice what they were meant to hold.

Before we got to Nepal, I did a deal with Ethan that if he wrote two pages in his diary each day, I would give him 500 rupees that he could use to buy sweets or souvenirs. As we climbed Namche hill, I explained to him that these porters were getting 500 rupees to carry these huge loads from Lukla to Namche, then I told him that the porters had to use that money to pay for somewhere to live and all the food for themselves and their families.

This shocked Ethan but it also helped him to understand how fortunate we are. 'Wow, Dad, that's terrible that they have to do all that to earn 500 rupees, when all I have to do is write in my diary.'

A bit over halfway up the hill, there's a lookout from which you can see Mount Everest. The previous times I'd done this trek, I had been a bit superstitious about not looking at the mountain. This time, though, it was so special to be there with Ethan when he got his first glimpse of Everest away in the distance, a huge white cloud bloom trailing off the southern ridge. The sheer power and strength of the mountain is just awe-inspiring.

As we stood and looked out at Everest, Ethan had heaps of questions. 'Which way did you go, Dad? What's that mountain over there? Why is all that cloud coming off it? Is anyone on Everest now?'

I did my best to answer all of them as we made the most of a break to catch our breath.

From there we climbed on and were happy when we eventually made it to Namche Bazaar, which is the largest Sherpa village in the Khumbu region. It's a beautiful town, dotted with red- and green-roofed homes and tea houses all built out of granite. As the gateway to the high Himalaya, the town is very popular with trekkers and climbers, many of whom use it as a spot to acclimatise to altitude. When Ethan and I arrived, the place was bustling as it was Everest climbing season.

Dr Rob had told me to stay in a little family-run place

called Namaste Lodge, owned by Palden Sherpa. He was very friendly and gave us a great room with an amazing view out to the Himalaya. Palden was concerned about Ethan acclimatising so he recommended that, instead of going exploring, we should sit for a while and drink tea. I was a bit worried that Ethan might get bored, but before long he had his little chess set out and was happily playing against Palden and some of his Sherpa friends.

The following day, I had planned to trek over the hill to Khumjung Village, but Palden had other ideas. He said, 'No way. Rest, Mike. You don't know how tired Ethan really is.'

It's amazing that local kids make this trek every day, even when it's snowing, just to get to high school.

Palden had lived his whole life there and had seen many trekkers come through, so I trusted his advice. Ethan and I spent the day exploring Namche instead. We found a really cool bookshop where we got chatting to Nima, the shop's owner. Before long, he offered Ethan a chance to play with the flight simulator on his computer. Ethan was in heaven and this was the start of my friendship with Nima.

While Ethan played, Nima and I chatted. He told me that his parents had borrowed money to help his brother train to be a pilot. I couldn't imagine what it must have taken for a boy from Namche to train to be a pilot. Over the years, I've kept in touch with Nima and the last I heard his brother had a job piloting those flights in and out of Lukla. Just amazing!

The following morning, we left Namaste Lodge feeling well rested. It was time to trek over the hill to Khumjung—

and, when I say hill, I mean steep hill. It's amazing that local kids make this trek every day, even when it's snowing, just to get to high school. While those local kids take an hour to get across the hill, it took us about four hours to get to Khumjung. I had a special reason to take Ethan there. Built in 1961, the local school was the first to be funded by Sir Edmund Hillary's Himalayan Trust.

As we approached the top of the hill before our descent into Khumjung, we had the most spectacular view of Ama Dablam and Mount Everest. Ethan and I just sat there for about half an hour, as he asked a whole lot more questions about Everest and Ama Dablam. It was so cool just being there together, chatting away.

We arrived in Khumjung only to find that all the government workers were on strike for the day, so the school was closed. Luckily, one of the teachers was there anyway, and when he saw Ethan, he came out to say hello. We explained who we were and where we were from, and the teacher happily showed us around, taking us to see the first classroom Sir Ed built. It still looked exactly the same as it did in the photos I'd seen of it from 1961.

After our little tour of the school, Ethan and I went and had some lunch at a local cafe. We both had some noodles, and when we finished Ethan asked if he could have a milkshake. He'd been having a few issues eating as he didn't like the local food much. I asked the staff about the milk powder and water they used and it all sounded OK so I ordered him one. Ethan drank it down quickly, saying it was really good. Then we headed off back to Namche, arriving just in time for dinner.

Ethan had a good feed of roast chicken and went to bed

early. It had been a long day for both of us and I'd planned for us to head towards Pangboche the following day to see Lama Geshe if Ethan was feeling up to it.

Later that night, Ethan woke with a very sore tummy. As he disappeared to the toilet, I asked him not to flush it so I could see what was going on. I was really worried when I saw that, not only did he have diarrhoea, but there was blood in it.

If Ethan was going to be up all night, I was going to be right there with him. So, for the rest of the night, we made regular treks down the stairs to the bathroom.

The following morning, Ethan seemed a bit better, but I decided I'd rather be safe than sorry. My mate Dr Rob was up at base camp, preparing for a sixth ascent of Everest, so I phoned him for some advice. He asked me lots of questions. How bad were the cramps? What did the blood look like? Did he have a fever?

Fortunately, Ethan didn't have a fever, so Rob reckoned it was just a matter of letting the bug pass through his system. For me, it was a horrible time. Ethan didn't feel like eating or drinking anything, and I hated seeing him so weak and sick.

When it comes to travelling with kids, I always make sure I have access to a doctor by phone. Some travel insurance policies have this and it gives great peace of mind. If you're concerned about your child's health, don't wait to seek medical advice. Quite often you can stop a small problem from turning into a major issue if you deal with it straight away.

I was really relieved when Dr Rob said he was due to come down from base camp for a rest, so he would start the 50-kilometre trek that day to come and see us both in Namche. Now that is a good friend!

Since Rob and I had met on Everest back in 2007, he'd spent time staying with me and my family in Auckland. The kids absolutely loved him. He spent endless hours playing with them, wrestling or jumping on the trampoline. They weren't the only ones who took a shine to him, either; Wendy's friends seemed to find a lot of excuses to come and visit while he was staying. I can't imagine what they saw in this handsome, charming British doctor . . .

That evening, a young American woman arrived at the lodge. She talked to Ethan and me for ages, and it turned out she had been emailing some guy called Dr Rob about trekking and hadn't got any response. In the end, she had decided to just come to Nepal and trek on her own. I laughed and told her that we were due to meet the elusive Dr Rob the following day. The world is indeed very small.

When Dr Rob arrived, Ethan was over the moon to see him. He examined Ethan and recommended resting until the bug had gone from his system.

I took a bit of perverse pleasure in introducing our new American friend to Dr Rob. He was a bit embarrassed, but got over it quickly and the four of us spent the rest of the day hanging out and playing cards.

That evening, we were all sitting in the dining room and Ethan wasn't feeling the best, so he lay down and put his head on my knee. The American woman offered to rub his tummy to make him feel better, but he wasn't having a bar of that.

Over the next few days, Ethan slowly got better and we had a great time exploring Namche with Dr Rob. Then it came time to say goodbye. Ethan hugged Dr Rob and we set off down the valley towards Monjo. Then I noticed that

Ethan was crying. The tears flowed for about 20 minutes, and I tried to comfort him. He knew that Dr Rob was going back to climb Everest, and he knew that people got killed climbing. It was so hard for the young fella. It was also an eye-opener for me—there was no way I would ever climb Everest again while my kids were still young.

We took two days to get down to Lukla, then we flew back to Kathmandu. We spent another three days there, while Ethan did his best to spend all the money he'd earned writing in his diary. He amassed a good array of all the little trinkets that Kathmandu is famous for, and developed some excellent bargaining skills.

I'd explained the haggling process to Ethan and he was keen to try it. He was a bit shy at the first shop, but I insisted he go in on his own and told him I would wait outside. He did well, and the Nepalese just loved him. All the store keepers kept discounting their prices. By the end of the day, Ethan had worked out he could get stuff really cheap. He'd taken to haggling so well that I had to have a chat with him about what's fair. The Nepalese are kind-hearted people and they don't see many Western children, so they would almost give their goods away to Ethan, saying, 'You will bring me luck today!' When I realised what was happening, I told him that he wasn't allow to go below half the asking price.

▲

The whole trip with Ethan was special. The biggest reward for me was seeing the look on Ethan's face when we got home and he was telling the family stories about what he'd seen while we were away. I could tell he felt really special.

By the end of the day, Ethan had worked out he could get stuff really cheap. He'd taken to haggling so well that I had to have a chat with him about what's fair.

The trip hadn't been easy by any means, and there were times when I had been really worried that I'd done the wrong thing by bringing such a young child on such a big journey, especially when Ethan got sick. But the bond we developed over that time was really deep, and it made all of the worry absolutely worth it in the end. Hanging out together, just the two of us, for such a long period of time was just so cool. The words I'd read all those years ago in one of the Parents Inc books rang true: kids spell love T-I-M-E. It doesn't have to be as massive as trekking to see Everest, of course; it can be absolutely anything, as long as it's one on one.

CHAPTER 5
GUIDING
IN THE
HIMALAYA

The trip with Ethan also gave me the opportunity to have a look at all the logistics involved in running my little trekking business. While we were there I had a meeting with Iswari from Himalayan Guides, who would be helping me with all the planning. Officially, I was working for him, which meant I could avoid any red tape. I wanted my trips to be different from the usual trek up, tag Everest base camp and trek back down again. With Iswari's help, I employed some Sherpa who had climbed Everest and who lived in the villages that we would be visiting. The idea was that my team would not only hear my stories of Everest, but also have the opportunity to hear Sherpa stories and visit Sherpa homes.

I opened the first trip up to Air New Zealand staff and within four days it had sold out. The team was made up of people from all over the company, including the then-CEO, Rob Fyfe. I was a bit nervous taking the first team, not just because the CEO of the airline was there, but also because it was my first time guiding a team on a trek.

While Iswari had everything organised in Nepal, I had quite a lot to do to make sure everyone was ready for the trip. One of the key things I ensured that everyone do was talk to a doctor who specialised in travel medicine. That way I knew that everyone would be up to date with any vaccinations, and any other medical needs they might have in Nepal would be sorted.

When we arrived in Kathmandu, Iswari was there to meet us with flower necklaces for everyone on the team. As we drove to the hotel—we were staying at the Manaslu, of course—I loved seeing everyone's reactions to the busyness and colour of the streets of Kathmandu. They were all pretty excited to have a couple of days to explore the city before we flew up to Lukla.

After the normal hair-raising flight into Lukla, we met up with our two lead Sherpa: Ang Nuru and Nawang. I'd met Ang Nuru when I climbed Ama Dablam. He was born in Pangboche and had climbed Everest twice—once without oxygen. He had also climbed Cho Oyu, the sixth highest mountain in the world, 13 times. Nawang was also born in Pangboche. He had been on Everest in May 1996 when a blizzard trapped numerous climbers, leaving thirteen dead. During that storm, he had climbed up to Camp 4 to rescue several climbers.

With the two Sherpa, we all trekked up to Monjo for

the night. The next day we climbed the Namche hill. After two nights in Namche, we headed up to Pangboche. It's the hardest day of trekking, but this is where the Himalaya really open up. From here, we could see Everest and Ama Dablam towering into the sky. The views of these mountains reinvigorated everyone on the team.

In his opinion, it was neither human nor ape— it was, he believed, from an unknown species.

At Pangboche, I'd arranged for us to stay with my old climbing friend Gurman, who ran a guesthouse called Sonam Lodge. It was great to see him again. Once everyone was settled in, I asked Rob Fyfe to come with me to visit Lama Geshe.

▲

There was a very special reason that I wanted Rob to meet Lama Geshe before the rest of the team. At one of our team meetings before we left for Nepal, I'd told the group about the yeti remains that had been stolen from Pangboche, explaining that the village had suffered financially due to the disappearance of the artefacts. I'd done quite a lot of research into the story of the hand and skull, and how they went missing. According to the people of Pangboche, the artefacts had been in the village for centuries, but they weren't seen by any Westerners until the 1950s, when a yeti hunter called Peter Byrne was paid to lead an expedition to Nepal. There, Byrne examined both the skull and the hand and quickly came to the conclusion that the skull was fake. However, he was less certain about the origins of the hand. In his opinion, it was neither human nor ape—it was, he believed, from an unknown species. The monks refused to allow the hand to be taken away for testing, saying that it was very precious and bad things would happen to the village if it was ever taken away.

Along with a primatologist in the UK, Byrne hatched a plan to remove some of the fingers from the yeti hand and replace them with human fingers. Quite how he managed to do this is unclear—some suggest that Byrne got the monks drunk, but when I emailed him to enquire he told me that he'd paid them a lot of money to replace two of the fingers. Whatever the truth, the fingers were soon spirited out of the country.

The bones were then examined by specialists at a university in England, who pronounced them to have come from an undetermined species. The yeti hunters were happy. The monastery was happy—they still had their hand, and people would still visit them and pay a small donation to see the artefacts. In the 1960s, Ed Hillary visited while leading a yeti-hunting expedition. A doctor on his team confirmed that the hand had some human bones but that the others were of uncertain origin.

Then, in the early 1990s, a North American TV network broadcast a story on the yeti pieces and a short time later the artefacts were stolen—probably on order for a wealthy collector of antiquities. The monks and the local villagers were devastated.

When I was telling the Everest crew the yarn of the yeti hand and skull, I mentioned that I'd thought about getting some replicas made. I thought this might encourage people to go up to visit the monastery and thereby reinstate the monastery's income. Rob had offered to introduce me to multiple Oscar winner Sir Richard Taylor from Weta Workshop, home of the special effects for the Lord of the Rings films. 'Let's just put it out there, Mike,' Rob said.

I emailed Sir Richard, and he said he would love to help. I sent all the photos I could get of the hand and skull down to the team at Weta Workshop, and they got to work straight away. A week later, they called me to say that the replicas were both ready, so I flew down to collect them. I was absolutely stunned: they looked identical to the originals in the photographs. They really are miracle workers at Weta.

▲

The night before the whole team were due to visit the monastery, Rob and I went to see Lama Geshe. I wanted to make sure that it would be all right with the lama if we donated the replica yeti artefacts. I had brought them with me to Pangboche, stored carefully inside my pack.

Lama Geshe didn't seem too impressed to have his evening interrupted by us. When we showed him the artefacts, he had many questions. I was shocked to hear Lama Geshe ask, 'Why do we need these things? Our village is peaceful and content. They might bring trouble to this village.'

I panicked. Perhaps I had misjudged everything and made a terrible mistake. Perhaps these people were not interested in money and the lost income from the replicas wasn't that important to them after all.

Rob spoke to Lama Geshe at length, and after a while the lama started to come around to the idea of restoring the artefacts to the monastery, but he asked to be given time to think about it.

Before we left, I had something else I needed to ask of Lama Geshe. I explained to him that, since he had named our youngest son, our other two children had asked if he might give them names too. He said he would give it some thought.

The next day, Lama Geshe agreed to formally bless the skull and hand replicas before we took them to the monastery. Our team gathered at the lama's house and went inside for the blessing. As we entered his living room, we bowed our heads and each of us passed him a silk scarf with a small donation wrapped up in it. He then put the donation aside and placed the scarves around our necks. One by one, we touched heads with the lama as he chanted a mantra. It was very special. Once we were all seated, Ang Nuru interpreted for Lama Geshe and he said he was very grateful for the replica artefacts. I was relieved when he thanked me, saying no one else had ever thought to do such a thing for Pangboche.

He said he had never named a girl before; no high lama had ever done this. Maya would be the first.

He then blessed us with the same mantra he had chanted when he blessed me on Everest four years beforehand. I could feel the emotion inside me and a few tears started to flow.

With his daughter, Tashi, translating, Lama Geshe announced that Ethan's name would be Tsering Dorje—long life and strong like diamond. He then said he had never named a girl before; no high lama had ever done this. Maya would be the first. He named her Namkha Dolma—blue sky Green Tara (Green Tara is a Buddhist goddess).

After receiving Lama Geshe's blessing, we all went down to the monastery to present the artefacts to the lama there. News about the replicas had spread and a small crowd of locals had gathered. The team met with the monastery council and the formal handover took place. I pulled out the skull and presented it to the head lama of the monastery. He looked at it with great interest, then passed it down the line of council members. This was the real test as to how good the replicas were. The council members were astonished at the detail on the skull, pronouncing it to be just like the real one.

Then I brought out the replica yeti hand, which was small enough to store in a beautiful handmade Nepali wooden box with the words 'From your New Zealand friends' carved on the base. I lifted the lid and showed the head lama. His eyes opened wide and, as he held the hand up in the air, there was a gasp from some of the local people. He said something in Sherpa and Ang Nuru turned to me, saying, 'He is telling everyone you have brought the real hand back.'

I was shocked. 'No, no!' I said. 'Zuma, zuma!' meaning 'Fake, fake!'

The lama looked at me and I showed him that the hand was not made of real bone. He found it hard to believe as it was so much like the original. I explained how I hoped that it might restore a small income to his monastery from people making donations to view the artefacts. The lama thanked us all and we shared some tea.

Fully blessed and with our delivery made, the team carried on with the rest of our 14-day trek. During that time, we all made our way up to Everest base camp and back down again. Every single person was pushed to their limits—physically, mentally and emotionally. It was also a very special journey for everyone in a spiritual sense. That blessing from Lama Geshe had a profound effect on some members of the team, and years later people still talk about it.

I learned so much about people on that first base camp adventure. Being a leader at high altitude is a lot like parenting in some ways—sometimes you just need to take a deep breath and count to ten in your head. The problem might even resolve itself, making you look like a great leader!

▲

Wendy flew to Kathmandu to meet me and the team, and then the two of us had a few days together in Singapore as a couple. It was important that she had something exciting to look forward to as well.

When we arrived home I sat down with the kids. They were crawling all over my expedition bags, asking about presents from Nepal. I had brought them Buddha statues, prayer flags and a few little local toys like handmade *papier-mâché* puppies. They just loved them.

At dinner that night, I told them how I had asked Lama Geshe for names for Ethan and Maya. They listened intently, smiling when I told them each of their names. That evening, everyone called each other by their Sherpa names.

▲

The first trek to Everest with a team from Air New Zealand was so successful that it wasn't long before another was in the pipeline. Wendy was really involved, helping me plan these treks, and I loved knowing that she would be in

Kathmandu to meet me when we finished. This time would be different, though—this time she was bringing Maya, who had just turned seven.

I was excited to share such a special place with another group, but at the same time I needed a personal adventure, something as crazy as Everest, but without the chance of getting myself killed in an avalanche or crevasse fall. It also had to be short, as I didn't want my kids growing up with their dad away all the time.

My plan was to guide the team to Everest base camp and then stay the night there. I would then get up early and climb Kala Patthar, a small peak near Everest, where—at 5600 metres—I would begin my attempt to run the world's highest marathon. My route was to take me down from Kala Patthar to Lobuche, then to Dughla and over the Cho La Pass, which was almost as high as Kala Patthar. I would then head through Phortse before finishing at Pangboche, where I would meet the rest of the team. By my calculations, that would be 42.2 kilometres. I had no idea if I could do it as I had never run at altitude before, but there's a saying often heard on Everest: 'You don't know how strong you are until strong is your only option.' I wanted to test my strength again, to see if I still had it, but in a safer way than mountain climbing.

While I was working out the logistics for the second trek, I had an email from one of the lamas at Pangboche monastery. First, the lama thanked me for the replica yeti artefacts and said they were really helping as tourists were coming to the monastery again to see them. Then he went on to tell me that one of the village's stupas (monuments) had been destroyed by some Tibetans who had come across the mountains looking for riches.

Apparently, they believed that the stupas contained gold and precious dzi beads. Originally from Tibet, these beads are traditionally made from agate and etched with beautiful eye designs. In Tibetan culture, they are believed to have a very positive spiritual effect, especially when it comes to warding off bad luck. In 2010, my friend Palden Sherpa gave me a dzi bead that had been in his family for many generations. It is one of my most prized possessions and I have not taken it off since I was given it.

The reason for the lama's email was that, because I'd been so kind to the monastery before, they wanted to know whether I might be able to help them buy 600 kilograms of cement to rebuild the stupa. I was pretty sure I could come up with the money for the project—but how on earth would I get the cement to Pangboche when the nearest road was 350 kilometres away?

At the end of his email, the lama wrote the best sales pitch ever: 'If you help us, you will have a good next life.' How could I say no to that?

At the end of his email, the lama wrote the best sales pitch ever: 'If you help us, you will have a good next life.' How could I say no to that?

After some quick calculations and a couple of conversations with people on the ground in Nepal, I worked out that airlifting the cement by helicopter was the only answer. Then there was the small matter of getting it carried the 20 kilometres from the airfield to the village. That was going to cost $100 per bag.

I sent an email to the first team I'd taken to Everest—and,

of course, I finished it off with the words 'If you help us, you will have a good next life.' With their help, the cost of transporting the cement was raised within two hours!

I sent the money to Nawang Sherpa, who later sent me photos of the cement coming off the helicopter and of the porters carrying the bags up to Pangboche.

Nawang also told me that the lama wanted to make a plaque on the side of the stupa thanking me and the team. I said no, but thank you for the offer; just walking past that first stupa near the entrance of Pangboche and knowing we had helped would be enough.

The second trek was really nice. The team members were all great and I was a little more confident in my ability as a trek leader. Together we made our way to base camp— stopping at Pangboche for a blessing along the way.

At base camp, the Sherpa had set up our tents along with our own toilet and cooking tent. Dinner that night was a simple Rara noodle soup followed by hot tea or hot chocolate. (It sounds exotic, but Rara is simply a Nepalese brand of instant noodles!)

Staying a night at base camp is quite an experience, as you are camping on the glacier and it slowly moves, creaks and groans. All night you can hear avalanches in the distance— some small and quiet, and others so loud you think that they are about to hit your tent. When I'm there, I wear ear plugs pushed in really tight so I can sleep, but for the clients it's really exciting.

The next morning, the team were going to trek up Kala Patthar, the peak where I'd be starting my run. I got up a couple of hours before them and set off with Ang Nuru Sherpa. I felt comfortable leaving the rest of the group, as they were accompanied by four Sherpa guides and four porters.

Ang Nuru took a direct line up the mountain, as there was absolutely no path. We were just making it up as we went along. I asked Ang Nuru a few times if the team would be coming up this way. He assured me they wouldn't as it was too difficult for them. It took about an hour and a half to reach the top, and we got there just as dawn was breaking.

After a bit of a warm-up, there was nothing else for me to do but start running. I was scared, and I wasn't sure if I could do it. This really was a leap of faith.

Ang Nuru ran with me all the way to the Cho La Pass. It was about there that I realised the cold had affected the battery on my GPS watch and it had died around the 23-kilometre mark. I was gutted, as I needed the GPS data to present to the Guinness world record people. I still had my SPOT tracker (a satellite personal messenger), but the data from this wasn't accurate enough to provide the proof they needed. If I did set a world record today, it would be an unofficial one—but, as I tell the kids all the time, just because things get tough, you should never give up.

During my run, my SPOT tracker worked well, updating every few minutes. Laid over a satellite map, my route looked very impressive. Wendy and the kids could actually see where I was in the Himalaya in real time.

We stopped at the top of the pass and Ang Nuru pointed out two rocks far in the distance and told me that was where I needed to go. His demeanour changed a little, and I could tell he was worried for my safety. He told me to go straight and go fast, then he gave me a hug and asked me to be careful. He then turned back towards Kala Patthar, where he would meet the rest of the team and guide them back to Pangboche.

From there, I set off on my own, a little scared. For the next six hours, I didn't see another living person. It was difficult to run and give it my all when there was no fixed finish line. I went into survival mode, and moved as fast as I could.

After another three hours I found a little tea house and the lady there asked if I was Mike. My friend Gurman had been planning to meet me there and guide me back to Pangboche, but he had left half an hour before I got there. I figured I'd catch up with him in Phortse, the next village along, which I thought was about ten minutes away. 'Oh no,' the lady said. 'It's at least two and a half hours away.' My heart sank.

By 6pm, I was still running. I still had food and water, and I was able to keep warm but, when night fell, I started to worry. Thick cloud rolled in and I could only see a few metres in front of me. It got dark very quickly.

The night was so black that there was no difference between having my eyes closed tight or open wide. I had a head torch with me but, since I'd started running in the dark that morning, the batteries had gone flat. Thankfully, I had a small emergency LED light, but I knew the battery on it wouldn't last long. I'd been on the move for 15 hours by this time and things were getting serious. I knew I was starting to stagger a bit, and I could easily slip off the track and fall to my death. I didn't know where I was, but my SPOT tracker was telling everyone at home my exact location. At least if I fell off the track they would find me — dead or alive. Probably dead.

As I ran, I tried not to think about the yeti. I'm not sure if I fully believe in the yeti, but it would be fair to say that there is something out in the Himalaya that makes a very strange noise, leaves large tracks and scares the crap out of the locals.

My mind was a bit of a shambles. I thought that I'd be

fine if there were no rhododendrons around because legend has it that yeti love rhododendrons. But then I shined my little torch up and I was smack in the middle of a large rhododendron forest. 'There's no such thing as yetis. There's no such thing as yetis . . .' I took off.

> **I told the owner I'd come from Kala Patthar via the Cho La Pass. He said, 'Impossible. Not possible. I've never heard of anyone doing that and I've been here for 65 years.'**

It seemed like ages before the little lights of Phortse peeked through the clouds. I knocked on the door of a small house and asked for help. They took me to a little tea house, where I told the owner I'd come from Kala Patthar via the Cho La Pass. He said, 'Impossible. Not possible. I've never heard of anyone doing that and I've been here for 65 years.'

I didn't even know if I'd made the 42-kilometre distance, but I was totally shagged! I tried to ring my Sherpa friends, but the phone wouldn't work so I collapsed into bed with a thin blanket, wrapped some Air New Zealand and Vodafone flags around me and fell asleep despite the freezing cold.

The next morning, I got up and on the trail really early, as I knew my Sherpa friends would be worried about me. It was a spectacular day, with Ama Dablam towering above me in the clear blue sky. It was so good to be alive. About halfway back to Pangboche, a friend of Gurman's met me and walked the rest of the way with me.

Gurman was extremely happy to see me as he'd been very worried when I hadn't turned up the night before. I explained that I had missed him by only a few minutes and hadn't been able to catch him. I quickly called Wendy and Ang Nuru to let them know I was OK.

Wendy told me that the SPOT tracker showed that I'd done more than the necessary 42.2 kilometres so I was very happy. I had given it everything I had and that was good enough for me. It was more about the adventure than any official record. And I sure found the place I was looking for—I knew that I had what it took. I was strong!

Later that day, my trekking team arrived, all relieved to see me. They told me that Ang Nuru had been really worried when he heard that I hadn't met up with Gurman. One of the team said the normally smiling Ang Nuru wasn't happy at all and had been seriously concerned for me.

Before we left Pangboche, the team stopped to help paint the stupa that we'd funded the cement for. The lama was so grateful for our help. It was great to be able to do something for the village in such a visible fashion. There were two other stupas that looked quite rundown. Some of the locals told me that these stupas were over a thousand years old. I offered to help repair them, but was told that they were happy with them as they were. 'They are our heritage. But thank you.'

CHAPTER 6
MAYA

Ever since Ethan had come back from his seven-year-old trip, Maya had been making plans for her turn.

Having just turned seven before I left on the guided trek, the timing was perfect for her to come and meet me in Kathmandu with Wendy. The plan was that we would stay together for a few days in Kathmandu, then Wendy would fly home with the team while Maya and I headed off on our adventure.

I met them both at the airport. I was excited, but Maya was off the scale. She loved the drive into Kathmandu. As I'd done with Ethan, I checked us into our hotel then took Maya shopping. The Nepalese people just loved my girl and kept asking what her name was. When she said 'Maya' they'd say, 'No, no, your English name. Maya is a Nepalese name!' When she told them that Maya *was* her real name, they were rapt. In Nepalese, Maya means big love.

That night, the whole base camp team went out for a celebration dinner. Nawang brought his wife, Dolma, and their seven-year-old daughter, Kusang, with him. The two girls hit it off instantly. They soon started drawing pictures of their homes for each other. It was so cute hearing them explain their drawings. 'Here is my house. This is our yak. Here is my grandmother.' Then, 'This is my house. Here is my cat. These are my brothers and this is my pet turtle.'

A few days later, Maya and I waved Wendy and the trekking team goodbye, then started to get ready for our own trek. Even though I was a bit shattered, this was my time with Maya and I was determined to make it as good as possible for her.

Maya was pretty thrilled to fly into Lukla. As we took off from Kathmandu and climbed to cruise altitude, she looked out of the window at the snow-capped Himalaya and asked a whole lot of questions. Intriguingly, hers were quite different from Ethan's. 'Are they farms, Dad? What do they grow? How do people live on such steep mountains?'

Even though I was a bit shattered, this was my time with Maya and I was determined to make it as good as possible for her.

I explained how, over thousands of years, the Nepalese had built terraces on the sides of the mountains so they could farm. This just generated heaps more questions.

Once we landed, we went to see Dawa Sherpa at Paradise Lodge. Dawa made a real fuss over Maya, which she enjoyed immensely!

I don't give the kids a lot of rules when we're out trekking, but they know the key ones. As I told Ethan: when someone speaks to you, you look them in the eye and speak up. Maya was really good at this, but a few people wanted to squeeze her cheeks. She wasn't having a bar of that, and she would pull back and smile politely. People got the picture very quickly.

My other rules are pretty simple things, which I drummed into them after Ethan got sick—always wash your hands with soap and then use hand sanitiser (they each have their own bottle) before eating, and try not to put your fingers in or near your mouth.

After a bit of a rest at the lodge, we were off trekking. We walked along, chatting away until lunchtime. Maya was doing so well. We stopped for lunch in Phakding, where Ethan and I had stayed the night.

At lunch, Maya decided she wanted a Fanta. I'm really careful about what the kids drink while we're in Nepal, so it's bottled or boiled water only. Bottled fizzy is usually safe, though, so I bought her one.

Next thing, as she was eating her fried rice and sipping away on her Fanta, she suddenly threw up. She was very upset. It wasn't a big mess, but she was not happy. I was a bit worried, but as we were only at 2500 metres I was pretty sure it wasn't altitude sickness. While we'd been walking, I'd been getting her to drink as much as possible, since staying hydrated at altitude is very important. I think Maya might have just drunk too much fizzy; sometimes at altitude, fizzy drinks can expand in your tummy and I think this is what had happened with Maya.

I decided the best thing to do would be to stay put in Phakding for the night. That turned out to be a good decision as we both got a good night's sleep and Maya was a box of birds the next morning.

We started trekking early and Maya happily chatted away as we walked. My plan had been to stop the next night in Monjo, but as it was only 10am when we got there, we pushed on for Namche Bazaar. Climbing Namche hill was an amazing effort from Maya—she was so strong and determined, just like her mum!

As we walked, Maya liked to listen to music on a tiny speaker and we would both sing along. I would join in very enthusiastically when no one was around, which prompted quite a lot of laughter. Maya's nature is very caring and every time we stopped near some porters, she would give them some of our snacks.

Arriving in Namche, we were welcomed by Palden Sherpa at Namaste Lodge. Palden's wife, Tsering, took Maya away and gave her hands and face a good wash, just like a Sherpa kid. Palden asked where we had come from that day and when I told him we'd come all the way from Phakding, he said, 'Please, do nothing tomorrow. You don't know how tired she really is!'

I love the way my friends look out for my kids when we're in Nepal. I had no intention of ignoring Palden's advice.

After a day resting, we'd planned to head over the hill to Khumjung to visit the school there, but unfortunately the weather wasn't good enough. There were snow showers passing through—not the weather to take a seven-year-old on a full day's hike at altitude!

Maya was a bit annoyed, because she knew Ethan had been to Khumjung and she kept asking when it would be her turn to go over. I tried to explain that the weather wasn't good enough for us and that we would have to wait. She was very keen to push onwards and upwards, and I was amazed by her adventurous spirit.

Maya had another wish that I thought would be easier to grant—she wanted to see a real yak. She'd seen lots of yak-cow crosses, but not an actual yak. The Sherpa told me that if a yak goes below Namche they will die as it's too hot for them and they can't handle the low altitude.

Palden told us that there was a yak station right up at the very top of Namche and that was our best chance of seeing one, so Maya and I trekked up to the top of Namche in search of yaks. It was a 35-minute walk straight up!

At the top of the track, we came around a corner to find about 70 goats. They were all bleating and making these cute noises. There were mother goats, billy goats and heaps of kids. Maya got right in the middle of them all and two of the kids started to butt her gently as if playing with her. This put a huge smile on her face.

Maya looked at the goat-herd and asked, 'Where are they all going?'

The goat-herd understood and replied, 'Slaughter.'

I could see Maya thinking about it. She knew what slaughter meant in English, but she wasn't sure if the goat-herd had understood her.

Before she even had time to compute what was happening, I said, 'Slaughter is a little village about two hours away.'

She kept playing happily with the goats. Whew. I got away with that by the skin of my teeth.

Sometimes a tiny white lie or a little misdirection to avoid a potentially upsetting reality of life is needed when travelling. If Maya had found out that all those cute goats were destined to be goat curry in a few days, let's just say it would have caused a bit of drama. She would have spent the next week coming up with plans for us to rescue and adopt 70 goats.

We continued on our yak hunt, but we didn't find any, much to Maya's disappointment.

As we hadn't been able to make it to Khumjung, Palden arranged for Maya and me to visit the primary school in Namche, where the school bell was an old oxygen cylinder from Everest hanging on a rope; it was hit with a hammer to let the kids know when class was about to start. They made us really welcome and Maya stood in front of a huge class of Sherpa kids and spoke about life in New Zealand.

One of the things I have found about travelling with the kids is that it is vital to make sure they feel secure. I would go to bed at the same time as them and get up at the same time as them. I'd never, ever leave their side, no matter what we were doing.

The Sherpa children all wanted to know what pets Maya had, and when she said she had two turtles they were amazed. There aren't any turtles in the Himalaya!

That night, my friend Nima came to visit us at Palden's house. We chatted for a while and he suggested that we go to the pub for a game of pool. I refused, as I didn't want to leave Maya. One of the things I have found really important about travelling with the kids is that it is vital to make sure they feel secure. I would go to bed at the same time as them and get up at the same time as them. I'd never, ever leave their side, no matter what we were doing. I found this gave them the confidence to meet people and try things that they might find a bit scary. They could do it so long as they knew Dad was right there with them.

Nima said, 'Don't worry! Bring Maya with you. There is no age limit here, and she must have seen you drink a beer before. Let's go!' So off we went.

We got to the pub and two of Nima's friends took Maya off to play foosball in the corner. Before long, she was laughing and high-fiving them, and having a great time. It was so cool to see how confident and relaxed she was, and how comfortable she was in such a strange environment.

The following morning, we said our goodbyes to Palden and his family and headed down the valley. Maya was a little sad as she really enjoyed life in Namche. Palden and his family had made us feel so welcome. I could also sense she was a little annoyed that she hadn't got to go above Namche or see a yak.

Soon after leaving Namche, my lower back started to hurt. I had been carrying all the gear for both me and Maya, so my pack weighed about 27 kilograms. It was a bit heavy, but it was nice trekking with just the two of us without guides or porters. It also helped me to slow down to the pace of a seven-year-old.

As I readjusted the pack, a searing pain shot through my pelvis. It shocked me a little, as I'd never felt pain like it. We were at the bottom of the Namche hill and still about two or three hours from Phakding. I thought about it for a second, then told myself to harden up, before doing up the pack and carrying on. Soon, I began to feel very nauseous with the pain. I did my best to keep it from Maya as she was enjoying the walk. I didn't want her to think that I was hurting in any way as she might worry about her safety. I was 'it' for her—her whole world—while we were there. If for one second she thought I wouldn't be by her side or I was sick or unable to walk it would really worry her.

At the next little village, I took some painkillers and sat down for half an hour, sipping milk tea while I waited for them to kick in. Then Maya and I slowly trekked to where we would be staying the night. By this time I knew something was very wrong.

The following morning, things weren't any better, but we managed to make it to Lukla. I dropped the pack off at Paradise Lodge, where we would be staying the night before flying back to Kathmandu. Without the pack, I felt OK, but I was worried I had done some serious damage to my back.

Maya and I spent a few days in Kathmandu before flying home to New Zealand. Part of our family tradition is a huge welcome for the returning adventurers, and it was so cool to see Maya telling the whole family all about the trek. She and Ethan sat and swapped stories, while five-year-old Dylan enthusiastically talked about 'when it's my turn'.

For a long time afterwards, when I would tuck Maya into bed, we'd talk about our trip. I would ask her what she'd liked the most, then I'd sit back and listen to her talk. 'I loved Palden's house and Namche, all the little shops. I really liked Nawang. He is cool, Dad! Also the mountains are very big and cool with snow on the top. I like the yaks . . . but, Dad, we didn't see a real yak. I'm sad about that . . .'

I would ask if she wanted to go back, and her eyes would widen and light up: 'Oh yes, Dad, can we? When can we? Just you and me . . .'

CHAPTER 7

THE 777 PROJECT

Before I headed to Nepal for Maya's trip, I realised that it would be another couple of years before Dylan turned seven. I decided I needed a big goal to aim for during that time—something that would scare me, something that seemed almost impossible. As usual, it was a book that provided my inspiration. I read *Mad, Bad & Dangerous to Know* by the explorer Sir Ranulph Fiennes. In it he describes his mission with Mike Stroud to run seven marathons on seven continents in seven days.

That was it! Running a marathon on a new continent each day for a week was made all the more impossible by the fact I am a terrible runner. As far as I knew, only three people had ever done the 777—and none of them were New Zealanders. I was amped.

I decided I needed help from some other corporate sponsors. There was one company I tried hard to get on board, a large New Zealand vitamin company whose products I'd been taking for years. I thought they would be a perfect partner for the project, but I couldn't get them to even acknowledge an email. I was pretty frustrated about it, and I was telling another parent while watching Ethan play cricket one night.

I was a bit surprised when she said, 'We'll sponsor you, Mike.' I wondered if she really understood what she was promising me, but then she explained she worked for an international company called USANA, which makes pharmaceutical-grade health products. That was a very fortunate meeting, as the company has been a great supporter of mine ever since.

While I had my own goal to aim for, I also wanted this adventure to do some good for other people. I was thinking about possible charities to work with when Wendy suggested KidsCan. They provide thousands of New Zealand kids with breakfast, lunch, shoes, raincoats ... Anything to give them a better start in life. It was the perfect fit for me and they really understood what I was hoping to do. The 777 Project, as I chose to call it, was coming together nicely.

Ever since Lama Geshe had said to me, 'The world would be a much better place if everyone just gave a little more than they took', I've always looked for both big and small ways to give back to others.

Sponsors and charity on board, it was time to set some dates to work towards. I wanted to do it before the autumn fog set in on the Falkland Islands. There's only one flight a week to and from the islands, and the whole project depended on me making that flight. I was to start the week in the Falkland Islands (Antarctica), then fly to Santiago in Chile (South America), then on to Los Angeles (North America), then to London (Europe), then a hop across to Casablanca in Morocco (Africa), before heading to Hong Kong (Asia) and finally home to New Zealand (Australasia). Whew!

Everything was starting to fall into place, except for one thing—the actual running. The truth is that I wasn't a natural runner. Before my attempt at the world's highest marathon, I'd never run a marathon before. Hell, I'd never even run a half marathon before. The furthest I'd run was 16 kilometres!

Everything was starting to fall into place, except for one thing—the actual running.

In a way, the world's highest marathon attempt had been a bit of a trial run for The 777 Project in terms of proving to myself that I had what it took to tackle something truly crazy. It also gave me a chance to push my limits, believe in myself and not to worry about what other people thought.

When it came to preparing for The 777 Project, I did as much of my training as possible during school hours so the kids didn't miss having time with me. My work schedule made that possible, for which I will always be grateful. The training was huge. It took super focus, and I got really fit. Best of all, the project was only going to mean seven days plus a bit of travel time away from home.

While the risk of getting killed doing these marathons wasn't huge, I still felt the pressure of one big risk: failure. I believe that the possibility of failure has killed more dreams than all failures put together. Most people—including me in the past—are too scared to give things a go in case they fail. The result of that kind of thinking is that we fail before we even start—a lesson I soon came close to learning.

▲

With about two weeks to go until the date I'd set for my attempt at the 777, I began to get terrible nerve pain down my back and into my left glute. It was the same pain I had felt on the trek with Maya, when I was carrying the heavy pack. I tried to push through it, but eventually I realised I needed to see a doctor. That led to an appointment with a specialist, who sent me for an X-ray and an MRI scan.

The MRI results came through while I was talking to a journalist about the project. Wendy took the call and I could see she was crying. I knew instantly what that meant.

I tried not to think about what it might mean for the project—so many people had put in so much work to make it happen and I didn't want to let them down.

The MRI results came through while I was talking to a journalist about the project. Wendy took the call and I could see she was crying. I knew instantly what that meant. The test revealed a very significant stress fracture in my lower spine. I was devastated.

Once I'd cancelled the flights and hotels, called my sponsors and let the media know that the project was off, I felt like I'd failed—not only myself but all the people who'd helped me out, as well as all the kids I'd been trying to raise money for.

When I told our kids, they had lots of questions about my back. I showed them the X-ray and pointed to the place where the fracture was. You couldn't actually see it on the X-ray, but that didn't bother them. I think it was Dylan who said to me, 'Allsops never give up, eh, Dad?' I could feel tears welling up in my eyes. Then the words 'If you don't give up, you can't fail' came into my head. I realised that I didn't have to do The 777 Project immediately—I could put it off until I was physically strong again. Once I realised that, I relaxed a bit and focused on getting better. Thankfully, my sponsors were all still there alongside me and had promised they'd support me again when I was ready.

Eventually, after about six months, my back healed and I was ready to start running again. This time it was different, though. Instead of timing my runs, I just went out and focused on covering a certain distance each time. This seemed to reduce my stress and helped me to fall in love with running.

I was really fortunate to meet Lisa Tamati, a New Zealand ultra-distance runner. She had a bad back injury when she was a teenager, so she understood what I was going through. She really mentored me, and without her I probably wouldn't have even got to the start line of the first marathon. Having the right mentor to help you along can make a huge difference; they can sometimes take you beyond what you think you are capable of. Lisa did just that for me, and more.

▲

Before long, we were back into sorting out flights, hotels and running dates. The earlier I could schedule the run, the better, so I decided 16 February 2013 was the go date. I was happy to finally have a target to focus on, but slightly stressed that it only gave me three months to train. I told the kids about it and they didn't seem that interested—until I said that we would go to Disneyland when I came back! With all my adventures, I make sure there is something in it for everyone.

Through a whole lot of luck, planning and kindness from strangers, I managed to make all my flights, and I completed the first six runs in reasonable form. The one that mattered most to me, though, was my final marathon—from the airport into the centre of Auckland city.

Landing in Auckland, I couldn't wait to see Wendy. As I came out into the arrivals hall, I was so thrilled to spot her. I was transfixed—she looked stunning in a long, flowing dress. We hugged and I didn't want to let go. But there was a job to do: I still had a marathon to run.

With ten kilometres to go, Wendy was waiting to run the rest of the marathon with me. She had been training towards doing it and this would be the furthest she had ever run. I was so proud of her. We hugged and kept running. Shortly after, a little voice came from behind me, 'Mike, slow down!' It was Wendy. We both laughed. Me? Slow down? I was going really slowly as it was.

Eventually, Wendy got into the groove of it. We ran down Ponsonby Road, then down College Hill. With about six kilometres to go, my calf finally went into a full cramp and no amount of stretching helped. Wendy went over to the support car and pulled out some calcium and magnesium pills for me to chew. I munched away on them and slowly hobbled on. Five minutes later, my calf released and I started running freely again.

As I ran around Victoria Park, I could see more than 200 people waiting for me outside the Vodafone building. I started to feel this emotion welling up inside me. A complete stranger shouted, 'Go, Mike! Awesome stuff! Go! Go!' I felt tears rolling down my cheeks. I didn't want to show up at Vodafone crying, so I put my head down and ran as fast as I could to blow away the emotion.

After my little blowout I felt heaps better. The emotion had gone and I could simply enjoy the final few kilometres with my friends and supporters. With four kilometres to go, there was about 200 people running with me.

As I ran around Victoria Park, I could see more than 200 people waiting for me outside the Vodafone building.

As we got to the last kilometre, Ethan, Maya and Dylan joined Wendy and me so we could run the last little bit together. We had a family group hug, then Maya took off ahead and looked around the corner. 'Wow, Dad! There are HEAPS of people waiting for you!'

'OK, let's go. Let's finish it,' I said.

We let the rest of the runners get over the finish line first so the five of us could all do it together. It was pretty cool crossing the finish line with just my family around me. I was so proud. I'd missed them so much while I was away.

The route was lined with people cheering and clapping. I couldn't believe it was actually over. I had done it. All those flights, countries, miles upon miles of running, all the planning, logistics, sponsors, meetings, emails and Facebook updates. Wow. It was over.

The 777 Project was pretty cool in a number of ways. It fed my adventuring spirit. It was short, so there were no long trips away from home, and the whole family found it really exciting. Oh yeah, and we raised over $75,000 for KidsCan. And, as promised, the following week our family headed off to Disneyland.

CHAPTER 8

DYLAN AND ROBBY

Sometimes, the years feel like they roll on and on, but with our regular planning dinners and everything else that work and family threw at us, Wendy and I always seemed to be making the most out of life. Before long it was time to start planning Dylan's trip to see Everest with Dad. And he was excited—seriously excited. The topic of conversation would regularly turn towards his upcoming adventure. The cool thing was that he would often talk to his siblings and ask them questions. 'Did you carry your pack? Was it heavy? What is the food like?'

About a week before we left New Zealand to go to Nepal, there had been a devastating avalanche on the Khumbu icefall on Mount Everest on 18 April 2014. In the worst single disaster ever to have struck on the mountain, 16 Sherpa were killed. When I heard the news of the avalanche, I was really worried. I had many friends climbing at the time, including Dr Rob and his new wife, Dr Marie-Kristelle. I also knew that, since it was very early in the climbing season, there would have been a lot of people moving through the icefall. It didn't take long before both Rob and Marie-Kristelle checked in on Facebook to let people know they were OK. Modern technology is amazing.

For most of his life, Dylan had been hearing about Ethan and Maya's trips, so I was determined to make sure his was just as good as theirs.

Sadly, not all my friends had survived. One of the men killed was Pasang Sherpa. He lived in a small village just past Pangboche and I had met him on one of my Everest trips. We became friends on Facebook and we would like and comment on each other's posts. I was gutted when I heard of his death.

Once the extent of the disaster was known, a lot of my friends in New Zealand—especially the ones who had been to Nepal with me—asked what they could do to help. I started a small fund and raised about NZ$3000 that I planned to give directly to the families of the Sherpa who were killed when I took Dylan to see Everest.

For most of his life, Dylan had been hearing about Ethan and Maya's trips, so I was determined to make sure his was just as good as theirs. I had everything down pat by now: the flight, the airport pick-up, the hotel.

Everything ran smoothly for me and Dylan until we got to the airport for our flight from Kathmandu to Lukla. Apparently, there was fog at Lukla, so all travel was delayed. While Dylan and I were sitting waiting for the conditions to change, I got a call from Iswari. He told me that one of his helicopters was heading up to Lukla and there were seats available for Dylan and me if we wanted them. I said yes straight away—this was going to be a real adventure.

Iswari sent a Jeep over to pick us up and take us to the heliport. Thankfully, we hadn't checked in, so we still had our bags.

Right next to the heliport was a huge A330 aircraft. It had no engines, and the side and tail markings had been painted over. Even so, I could see that it was a Turkish Airlines plane.

Back in March 2015, the plane had been flying all night from Istanbul with 235 people on board. When it arrived in Kathmandu, the visibility was poor and the plane circled for more than an hour before making its approach, but the pilot pulled up at the last minute because he couldn't see the runway. After this missed approach, it is thought that the aircraft no longer had sufficient fuel on board to fly to an alternate airport. Kathmandu was the only option. On the next approach, some patches of fog rolled in and left the pilot with very little visibility. He landed the plane hard and it veered off the runway and into the grass between two of the airport's taxiways.

That no one was killed is a miracle. The grass was soggy after heaps of rain and this probably slowed the aircraft sufficiently to stop it from hitting the terminal. That said, the plane still managed to cause chaos, and the airport was closed for several days while plans were put in place to move the aircraft.

Dylan and I looked around the huge airliner, which was now stranded near the heliport. I had told him the story and a flurry of questions followed, but he seemed to take it all in his stride. We finished our inspection and hopped into the chopper with a few Sherpa who were also catching a lift up to Lukla.

Once strapped in, we took off and flew low over the wrecked A330 Airbus, then out over the packed, throbbing city of Kathmandu. From the air, we could see hundreds of trucks, buses and cars, and thousands of motorbikes.

Slowly, the city began to give way a little, and on the outskirts we flew over some huge brick factories, their chimneys smoking away as we passed. More and more land appeared between the houses. It was quite something to be flying over the terraces built into the steep terrain by Nepalese farmers. There were thousands of them. It's incredible to think that crops can be grown in these gardens, which almost hang from the foothills of the Himalaya.

The chopper flew low over the hills and passes, and the mountains got higher and higher. Then the haze cleared, and we could see the Himalaya all around us.

Just watching Dylan's face was pretty special. Initially, he just stared in complete awe, then his eyes started darting around. Then came the questions. 'Wow! Dad, look at that mountain. Is that Mount Everest? What's that village? Is that where we are going? How do they live on the side of the mountains like that, Dad?' It was cool seeing him so animated—just like Ethan and Maya had been.

Soon, Lukla airport come into view. Landing there is a totally different experience in a helicopter. In many ways, it is a lot safer and if I had the money I would chopper into Lukla every time.

It was also a strange experience. We were dropped off, and then the chopper flew away in a swirl of noise, dust and chaos. A few seconds later it was all quiet. I found myself standing there, thinking, *Gosh, we're here . . . What now?*

Dylan and I picked up our bags and went across to Paradise Lodge. The look of joy on Dawa Sherpa's face when she saw Dylan appear from behind me was so cool. 'Hello, Mike, and who is this little man?'

As we trekked along together, I realised just how different each of the kids are.

'This is Dylan,' I said, 'and it's his turn to see Everest with me.'

Dawa grinned and asked Dylan if he was hungry. He told her he was starving. We'd got up at 5.30am; it was now 11am and we'd only had a few snacks at the airport. We ordered eggs on toast and Dawa's famous sweet milk tea.

Brunch over and farewells to Dawa done, we started trekking at about midday. I wasn't sure how far we would get that afternoon but I was hoping to make it to Phakding by evening.

As we trekked along together, I realised just how different each of the kids are. Ethan was the trail blazer; when I took him I didn't really know what to expect. I had no idea how far we would get, whether he'd enjoy it or even whether I would enjoy it. With Ethan we talked quite a bit, but always seemed to end up doing times tables. With Maya, there was a little less talking, but the conversations seemed to be more thought out. We also listened to quite a bit of music.

It took me a wee while to work out how to make the trek as

enjoyable as possible for Dylan. The solution was to tell him stories about the area we were walking through. He listened intently and had lots of questions, so the conversations along the way were really cool. Dylan turned out to be a very deep thinker, and would consider his questions carefully. He seems to have an old soul, and he also has a very funny, very dry sense of humour.

The thing that intrigued Dylan the most was the yeti. I told him everything I knew—well, most of what I knew. I was careful not to tell him stories that were too scary, especially as we were in the Himalaya, the place of the yeti.

The Sherpa people don't like talking about yeti, so it's taken me about a decade of gentle coaxing, a few questions at a time, to find out much. One Sherpa told me that they don't like to talk about the yeti because every time someone sees one a person in their family gets really sick or dies.

This particular Sherpa told me that, a few years earlier, he'd been staying in a tiny stone hut while herding yaks way up in the mountains. One evening, it was snowing lightly as he returned to the hut. He cooked dinner and was just about to go to bed when he heard footsteps and noises outside. He was too scared to go out and look, as he knew the sounds were not made by any yak. Whatever was outside scratched on the hut's door and window before eventually giving up and going away.

In the morning, he went outside and saw footprints in the snow all around the small stone shack—footprints that disappeared into the distance in a straight line. They were very large and, according to the Sherpa, looked just like the famous yeti footprints English mountaineer Eric Shipton found at Everest base camp in 1951.

I asked if he followed the footsteps to see where the creature went, and he replied swiftly. 'No, Mike. I didn't. I locked myself in the shack and waited all day for new snow to fall so that I couldn't see where the tracks went. My people believe that if we see the yeti or evidence of it then someone will get sick in our family.'

The Sherpa also told me about his uncle's encounter with a yeti in Zonglha, near the Cho La pass. One night, there was a huge ruckus outside after the yaks had been tied up for the evening. The Sherpa came out of the lodge to see what was going on, only to find a big mess. The yaks had broken free and run off, except for one. It was dead. Its skull had been cracked straight down the middle, as if something had grabbed each horn and pulled so hard it broke in half.

As Dylan and I walked on, chatting about yeti, it started to get dark. We were nowhere near where I wanted to be.

As Dylan and I walked on, chatting about yeti, it started to get dark. We were nowhere near where I wanted to be. You can't rush or push a seven-year-old to walk faster. I did the same thing I'd done with the other two and let Dylan walk in front of me. He was very determined, especially when he found out that I had carried both Ethan's and Maya's packs some of the way. He wouldn't let me carry his pack—which contained his water and his rain gear—at all.

Not far from Phakding, I found a small tea house in a place called Ghat and asked the owner if we could stay the night. He was very happy to have us as guests and invited us to have dinner with him and his family that evening.

The whole family spoke good English and we had great conversations over dinner.

Dylan was happy with the food. The Sherpa make great dumplings called momos and he had some chicken curry and white rice followed by a can of Sprite and a Mars bar for dessert. He followed Dad's rules about looking people in the eye when they talk to you and speaking up. When he did this, he got a good reaction every time. 'Oh! What a polite young man you are.' As a result, Dylan naturally started speaking up and looking directly at people, which are pretty cool skills for a seven-year-old.

Dylan walked across the bridge like a confident little adventurer, dressed in his Icebreaker top and his buff around his neck. To be honest, he made my heart melt.

The following morning, we trekked all the way to Monjo, where we stayed the night before the big climb up Namche hill. The trick to tackling Namche hill is to get up early and be on the trail by 7.30am. Dylan and I set off early and entered the Sagarmatha National Park—Sagarmatha being the local name for Mount Everest. Here we presented our permits, which had been organised for us by Iswari. The army officers were impressed to see Dylan out trekking. They all talked to him and asked him plenty of questions. He happily answered them and enjoyed the attention.

For the next hour and a half, we walked along undulating trails before reaching a huge suspension bridge strung 150 metres in the air. It can be a little intimidating, but Dylan was fine. In fact, he found crossing it really thrilling.

The wind was blowing, and the suspension bridge was covered in colourful prayer flags. One string had come loose in the middle and was just attached at the ends. It was blown out in an arc, fluttering in the wind. Dylan walked across the bridge like a confident little adventurer, dressed in his Icebreaker top and his buff around his neck. To be honest, he made my heart melt.

We started making our way up Namche hill. The climb wasn't too bad as it was very busy with herds of goats, donkey trains and dzos (cow–yak hybrids) carrying loads of good up to Namche. All this activity kept Dylan entertained as we climbed.

Along the way, we stopped at the Everest lookout and I showed Dylan the mountain way off in the distance. His first question was, 'What's the big cloud of stuff coming off the top of it?' This was followed by 20 minutes of questions and answers on Everest and the atmosphere.

We were both happy to arrive at Namaste Lodge, where we were greeted like family by Palden Sherpa. He welcomed us in and sat us down and brought us sweet milk tea. Looking at Dylan, he said to me, 'This one is strong.'

There was a young boy in Palden's lodge called Robby. He was of the Rai ethnicity, who generally live in the east of Nepal, in the foothills of the Himalaya. Whereas the Sherpa people live in the mountains, Rai people come from lower altitude areas so they tend to be porters or cooks on expeditions.

If you're wondering how a Rai boy ended up being called Robby, there's a very sad story behind it. My friend Dr Rob found the boy working as a porter on Namche hill. When Rob first met him, he was carrying a huge load of goods weighing more than he did. It didn't take long for Dr Rob to realise that this was just a young child, so he helped the boy carry his load to Namche, then took him to Palden's house. There Dr Rob fixed his feet and found out he was an orphan. His father had died many years ago and his mother had, as Robby put it, 'walked off into the trees and was never seen again'.

Palden and Dr Rob came up with a plan that saw Robby live with Palden while Dr Rob paid for his school costs. Their generosity probably saved the life of the severely undernourished boy.

Despite a seven-year age difference between them, Dylan and Robby were about the same size, such was the impact of the older boy's tough start in life. The pair of them hit it off in a massive way. They played cards together, they challenged each other to games of chess, and Robby taught Dylan some Sherpa games. He also took Dylan and me up to the local school, where the two kids played on the swings and slide and ran around with a ball. It probably wasn't the ideal way to acclimatise, having just arrived at a higher altitude, but I couldn't say no—they were having so much fun. I just hoped Dylan wouldn't get too tired.

As we walked back down to Palden's place, I could see this lovely friendship forming between Robby, a Nepalese orphan, and Dylan, a kid from New Zealand. They stopped on the way down and Dylan held out a small necklace he had bought in Kathmandu and asked Robby what the designs on it meant.

Robby said, 'This is *Om mani padme hum.*'

'What does that mean?' Dylan asked, fascinated. He had a huge smile on his face.

Robby replied, 'It is Buddha's mantra. I don't know how to say in English.'

The pair of them laughed with each other and trotted off down the hill together.

Over the years, Wendy and I have copped a bit of flak for taking the kids on these big adventures, especially the Nepal trips. In reality, what we do on these trips is very safe.

As I watched them, I started thinking about the adventures I'd had with my kids. Given I hadn't had a dad to show me how to be a good father, I figured that maybe I wasn't doing too badly at the whole being a dad thing.

Over the years, Wendy and I have copped a bit of flak for taking the kids on these big adventures, especially the Nepal trips. In reality, what we do on these trips is very safe. It's just that the thought of going on trips like this is quite far outside some people's comfort zones. I reckon those people are missing the point—it's important to challenge what's comfortable, and Wendy and I want our kids to be able to do that. We also want them to learn that, unless it's someone they respect and trust, then other people's opinions of them don't matter at all.

Anyway, I was loving this time with Dylan. We stayed with Palden for three nights, then headed over to Khumjung School. This time the school was open.

Robby had told us he was in Room 16, which turned out to be the first classroom that Ed Hillary ever built. We walked over to the building just as the bell rang for the lunchtime break. Right then, about a thousand kids piled out into the school grounds, churning up huge amounts of dust, kicking footballs and chattering as they went.

Robby saw Dylan and ran over, putting an arm around his new mate and taking him into the classroom. Dylan pulled out some cards and they started playing a Sherpa game with some other kids—all right there in Sir Ed's first classroom. It meant heaps to me.

Dylan played with about five kids for all of the lunch break, while I wandered off and chatted with a few teachers. Everyone was really friendly and they were happy to meet another Kiwi.

When the bell rang for the kids to go back to class, Robby walked Dylan out of the classroom with his arm around him. They said goodbye, and we turned and headed away.

I asked Dylan if he was OK and he said he was. I could tell he was a bit choked up, but I didn't push it any further. I knew he was sad because he was going to miss his new friend.

CHAPTER 9

GOING FURTHER

With the other two kids, I'd trekked as far as Namche Bazaar. This time with Dylan, I decided we'd do something a bit different and head to a little village called Kyangjuma for the night, which is a few hours' trek from Khumjung. I wanted Dylan to meet a Sherpa lady there called Tashi. I had met her the first time I went to Everest base camp, and ever since then I have always stopped to have some sweet milk tea with her at Ama Dablam Lodge.

She'd heard me talk about my kids a lot, so she was really happy to meet Dylan. Then her eyes welled up and she looked at me and said, 'Mike, my son died in America.' It was heart-breaking to hear. I gave her a big hug and told her how sorry I was.

Later, someone told me he had been studying in the US

and passed away as a result of a heart condition. He was only in his twenties when he died.

Tashi told me that all the monks and lamas had come down from the nearby Tengboche Monastery for a special puja ceremony to mark 45 days since her son's death, which was to take place in two days' time.

Tashi took Dylan and me to her house. At one end there was a small monastery with about 20 monks and lamas, who were chanting mantras and playing Tibetan trumpets and drums. Dylan's eyes almost popped out of his head. I explained what was happening, and Dylan was very respectful and sat quietly and watched.

Afterwards, Dylan and I settled into our room, which had an en suite with a Western toilet—a bit of a luxury in the Himalaya. Tashi invited us to have dinner with her, so that evening, we sat in the main dining area with her and all the monks. Some of them spoke very good English and I explained to them that one of Dylan's names was Dalha, and that he had been named by Lama Geshe. They then translated in Sherpa for their companions, who would sneak a look at Dylan and smile or chuckle away. Dylan thought it was all pretty cool and smiled at the monks. He seemed to be at ease in their presence; he didn't hide behind me or anything. When they spoke to him, he answered very politely and had a little conversation with a couple of them.

The following morning, we sat outside and ate breakfast with a spectacular view of Ama Dablam. It didn't take long before Dylan had some company in the form of Tashi's Tibetan mastiff, Maya. Dylan found it rather hilarious that the dog had the same name as his sister.

Maya the dog just adored Dylan and followed him

around everywhere. In fact, on the whole trip animals seemed to gravitate towards Dylan. Dogs and cats would come straight up to him and want a pat. Some donkeys would uncharacteristically stop and look at him, and even the odd dzo would check him out. The Sherpa believe in reincarnation, so perhaps these animals saw something they recognised in Dylan.

In the morning, we hugged Tashi goodbye and set off back to Namche. It was only about a three-hour walk, so we trekked along, chatting away, and stopped at a few lookouts to take in the amazing views of Everest.

When we arrived back at Palden's place, it felt a bit like coming home. The welcome is always so nice there. He makes sure we sit and have tea before anything else happens. It's a very traditional way of meeting guests.

Dylan wasted no time asking Palden where his mate Robby was, and was disappointed to find out that Robby was away for a couple of days.

I spoke to Palden about the avalanche on the Khumbu icefall. He told me that he knew every single Sherpa who had been killed on the mountain that day. It's a very small community. Dylan knew what had happened, but didn't really understand the enormity of it.

The following day, Palden, Dylan and I went up to the local monastery to receive a blessing from Lama Fu. Dylan went first. He sat in front of the lama while mantras were chanted, then had rice and water sprinkled over him. The whole ceremony took about 20 minutes, and I was really proud of the way Dylan sat there so respectfully, focusing directly on the lama the whole time. Afterwards, we thanked the lama and headed back to Namche.

I spent the afternoon in Namche at Cafe de 8848, which belongs to my friend Nima, who I'd met on the earlier trip with Ethan. I sat and chatted with Nima while Dylan went off to do some shopping. It was really safe—I could see every step he took from the vantage point of Nima's balcony!

While I watched Dylan go from shop to shop doing a little haggling, I could see his confidence and his independence growing.

While Ethan had taken to haggling like a duck to water, Dylan took a while to warm to it. At first he wanted me to come along and help him, but I told him that this was all part of the adventure and he would have to work it out for himself. I taught him that he should ask to see things, try them on and then barter over the price.

The shops are full from floor to ceiling with colourful stuff—masks, jackets, necklaces, traditional souvenirs, you name it. But, best of all for me, there were no sweets to tempt Dylan! He would walk in and the Sherpa store keeper would help him try things on and answer his questions, but there was never any pressure to buy. While I watched Dylan go from shop to shop doing a little haggling, I could see his confidence and his independence growing. He came back with his purchases and told me all about them. It was clear he was proud of his solo shopping efforts.

The following morning, we said goodbye to Palden and his family, then set off back down to Lukla. We'd spent a bit longer in Namche than I'd initially planned and we needed to get to Lukla in one day. The walk from Namche to Lukla in a single day is huge for an adult, even one who has just climbed Everest and is super fit and acclimatised. While Sherpa children do it all the time, I wasn't sure how Dylan was going to manage it. To get around this, I organised for Dylan to ride a horse from halfway down the valley while I walked beside him.

Walking down Namche hill is great as you get to see all the trekkers puffing their way up. It is nice when someone gives you a little encouragement when you are on the way up, so I always make a point of saying things like, 'Well done! Keep going . . .' It sounds cheesy, but it makes a big difference. The biggest problem I had was keeping Dylan from going too fast. He was now acclimatised to the altitude, fit and motivated, so he was off ahead of me all the time.

We crossed back over the beautiful swing bridge and out of the national park, where a soldier was checking people's permits. He asked me to take a photo of him and Dylan, which my boy thought was pretty cool. Then we carried on to Monjo, where we stopped for tea and hot chocolate.

The horse turned up just outside Phakding, when we had about eight kilometres to go. Distances don't mean anything up there—the four kilometres up Namche hill can take up to seven hours to cover, so I knew we were at least four hours from Lukla when the horse arrived.

It was a small horse with a beautiful Tibetan blanket, a nice saddle and colourful reins. Dylan thought it was great. He happily climbed onto the horse and we set off, with the horse's owner leading it on a separate rein from the one Dylan held.

It didn't take long for me to start thinking the pace was going to kill me. I was carrying all the gear, as I had with the other two kids. This slowed me down to a child's pace, but now, oh my god! My heart felt like it was going to pop out of my chest.

I had to ask the horse's owner to slow down, but he wouldn't. He just kept going at the same pace. Every now and then, he would let me catch up, then he'd take off again. This went on for pretty much the rest of the day. The thing that worried me the most was that Dylan was out of my sight sometimes, but nothing I said made any difference. Thankfully, Dylan was having an absolute ball riding down the hill and didn't even realise that I was struggling. Needless to say, I had to take a few deep breaths and bite my tongue a little when I handed the horse owner his money at the end of the day!

In Lukla, we stayed a night with Dawa at Paradise Lodge and had her spectacular sizzling chicken. I had a couple of Everest beers and Dylan and I played cards with some of the Sherpa. Thankfully, I'd booked the 10am flight the following morning, which meant that I had a chance to sleep in after my exertions coming down from Namche.

Then, at 7am, Dylan and I were both woken by the roar of a propeller turbine engine in full reverse right outside our window. Dylan pulled back the curtains and his mouth dropped open. 'Dad, the runway is just there!'

He was right—the plane was about ten metres from our room. Ten minutes later, there was another plane, then another. There went my sleep-in!

The early wake-up did give us the chance to go into the village and do a little shopping between breakfast and our flight, though, so we made the most of it.

When we headed over to the airport to check in, it was chaos. There were shouting people everywhere and bags going all over the place. Thankfully, Dawa's husband was working on one of the check-in counters and he ushered us over. He weighed our luggage—and then us—and sent us to another counter where a soldier searched our bags. From there, we went through a metal detector on our way to security, where I was given a personal pat down. Let's just say the Nepalese take aviation security very seriously. They didn't frisk Dylan, though. Instead the guard knelt down, smiled at him and said, 'What's your name, young man? Where are you from?' Dylan replied and the agent said, 'You look very strong. Good man. Off you go!'

While the flight into Lukla is nerve-wracking, the flight out is pretty exhilarating too. As you taxi out to the start of the runway, the pilots edge the aircraft as close to the wall of the terminal as possible, lining it up as the runway disappears out of sight due to the 16-degree downwards slope. They then apply full power and hold the aircraft there for a few seconds to do a power check and make sure the engines are running OK. The brakes are then released and the aircraft is off, hurtling down the 400-metre-long runway with a 900-metre drop off at the end of it. They don't really pull back or rotate, as we say in the airline industry; it's more like they just let the aircraft fly itself off the runway!

We landed in Kathmandu in the familiar haze of pollution. The city sits in a bowl surrounded by mountains and all the smoke from the vehicles and industry doesn't really have anywhere to go. It's such a contrast to the mountains, where you can see for miles and miles and the air is so fresh and beautiful. That said, Kathmandu does have its charms. It's a wild, exciting place. Even though I've been there many times, I always find something new and surprising on each visit.

The day we arrived back in Kathmandu, Iswari had organised two Sherpa families to come into his office, so that I could personally give them the money that had been donated following the avalanche. Dylan was there with me and I explained that these families had lost their loved ones. It was hard for him to understand.

I recognised one of the boys there immediately. I'd met him on both of my Everest base camp treks. Both times we'd seen him carrying water on his back for his mother, and both times some of my team members had their photos taken with him. I didn't know at the time that he was the son of my friend, Pasang. Dylan played with him, showing him a card trick that he'd learned from Palden.

Talking to the family, I found out that Pasang's mother lived on her own in Upper Pangboche. I was devastated when I heard that she had lost her father, her husband and two of her three sons on Everest already. Pasang was the last one to be killed. It's hard to even think about a single person experiencing such loss.

I made sure that some of the money was given to her. When she received it via Nawang, she went straight to the monastery and donated the money to them for a blessing for her last son. Three months later, she died.

That evening, Iswari invited Dylan and me for dinner at his house with Rob and Marie-Kristelle, and another Kiwi mountaineer, Russell Brice. I was a bit nervous to meet Russell as he's an Everest climbing legend. He first went to Everest in 1974 and has climbed it twice, but he's most famous for being the first person to climb the Three Pinnacles on Everest's Northeast Ridge in 1988. The pinnacles were known as the last of the unclimbed great obstacles on the mountain.

When we got to Iswari's place, Dylan was pleased to see Dr Rob again, but quickly disappeared to play with Iswari's kids. It was one of the only times Dylan was out of my sight on the whole trip.

After the avalanche, a lot of Sherpa wanted to cancel that year's climbing and close the mountain.

While the kids were playing, Dr Rob talked a bit about the disastrous avalanche. He told us about one young Sherpa who was on his first Everest expedition. He had been in the avalanche, but had somehow managed to survive. When he finally made it back to base camp, his employer really looked after him and asked if he wanted to stay and wait to climb again. If not, he would be paid half his season's pay and could go home. He chose to return to his family as he was very shaken. The day after he got home, he was struck by lightning and killed. It's an unbelievably sad story, and I can't help but think that someone wanted him in a higher place.

After the avalanche, a lot of Sherpa wanted to cancel that year's climbing and close the mountain. Some expeditions left and some stayed. I think some teams preferred to leave it up to their own Sherpa to decide if they wanted to climb or not. It must have been pretty tense, given these company's clients would have paid upwards of US$100,000 to do the climb.

Eventually, the Nepalese government sent an official to Everest base camp. Given it takes ten days to acclimatise, they had to do some quick thinking. The officials flew there in a helicopter and, while on supplementary oxygen, they spoke to a huge crowd of Sherpa. If the oxygen had failed, they would have been unconscious in three or four minutes, so it was a gutsy thing to do. The upshot of the meeting was that the Sherpa wanted better and safer working conditions and they also wanted the mountain closed for the rest of that year out of respect for their fallen friends. The closure took place immediately. The Nepalese government offered all of the climbers affected by the closure that year a free permit in the future. Permits cost US$70,000 and each one can cover up to seven climbers.

The rest of the evening disappeared in a blur of high-altitude chat among Rob, Marie-Kristelle, Russell, Iswari and me. It was great to be among all these mountaineers, but I didn't miss the risk of climbing at that altitude. I was happy with the decision I'd made to put my family first.

After a couple more days in Kathmandu—where Dylan got to swim in the Hotel Manaslu pool whenever he wanted, unlike his older brother—it was time to say farewell Rob and Marie-Kristelle. It's always hard for me to say goodbye to Rob, as he is one of my closest friends. Even though I sometimes don't see him for years, when we do get together it's like we've never been apart.

▲

When Dylan and I landed in Singapore, we found that our luggage had been left in Kathmandu as part of an effort to reduce the weight of the aircraft. It seems to happen to me every time I travel back from Nepal, so I knew the routine.

We were flying with Singapore Airlines, and I was aware they had a policy that passengers whose luggage gets offloaded are to be paid compensation of SG$217 (NZ$235). I also knew that, if we didn't ask for it, we wouldn't be given it. I made sure to tell as many people as I could about the compensation for their stranded bags, which probably didn't thrill the customer service people.

When it was our turn to lodge a claim for our missing bags, the customer service agent got her own back, though! She gave me a form and the $217 in cash. I asked where Dylan's compensation was, as his bag had been offloaded too.

The agent looked straight at Dylan and said, 'Can you sign your name here, please, darling?' Dylan signed the form.

The agent then said to him, 'Now, put your hand out.'

I watched as she slowly counted $217 into Dylan's little hand and said, 'This is all yours, OK? It's not your dad's. It's all yours.' She looked at me and gave me a big, cheeky grin.

Dylan was beaming. He turned to me and said, 'Is this really all mine, Dad?' He couldn't believe it.

I knew I couldn't take it off him, so I winked and said, 'Yep, it's all yours!'

He was stoked. 'Wow, Dad. Singapore Airlines is so nice. I'm going to buy some presents with this.'

I've got to say, I loved that his first thought was to spend it on other people.

We filled in the rest of the day exploring Singapore, doing some shopping and just relaxing. Dylan seemed to take Singapore in his stride, just as he had Nepal. I took him to one of those places where you put your feet in the water and fish nibble the dead skin off your feet. I had my waterproof Samsung Galaxy phone with me so I dipped it in the water and filmed the fish pecking away at Dylan's feet, which was pretty classic. However, Dylan reckoned that every time I put my feet in the water all the fish left him and came charging over to my bigger, smellier feet!

Eventually, we were reunited with our luggage and it was time to head back to New Zealand. Landing in Auckland, all of the family were there to meet Dylan, the returning hero, just as they had been with the other kids.

Everyone sat around and listened to his stories, and he was especially proud that he had gone further up the valley than the other two. He was also proud that he had carried his backpack the whole way.

I was really happy that I had been able to follow through on my promise to take each of our children to see Everest with me, their dad, when they were seven. Each time I went, I'd turned down requests from other people who wanted to join us on our adventures, but it was important to me that it just be the two of us each time. I wanted these trips to be something my children could look back on as precious time with their dad.

At the time of the trips, it might not have seemed particularly special to them, as it was just what they did when they turned seven. But one day when they're older I'm sure they will see how massive it was.

There is one other thing I would say about taking a child into the Himalaya. I had enough experience in the mountains to feel comfortable taking my kids at age seven, but I wouldn't do that unless you really know what you are doing. If you're not an experienced trekker, I wouldn't take a child any younger than ten.

CHAPTER 10
A FAMILY ADVENTURE

At our next dreaming dinner at Taiko, Wendy told me that she really wanted us all to go up the Everest valley as a family to visit Lama Geshe. I couldn't believe my ears. At first, I wondered if she'd had a bit too much sake, but I soon realised she was serious. I was fizzing at the thought of showing Wendy the places she'd only heard stories about, and I couldn't wait to take everyone to see Lama Geshe.

I started planning the trip straight away, but first I had another little trip I needed to organise. Wendy's parents were going to the UK to visit her brother, BJ. From there, the three of them were heading to Paris for a few days. I knew Wendy would love to join them, so I decided to do something about it. Having talked to her mum, Lorraine, I booked Wendy on a flight to London and then Paris, so she could surprise her dad and her brother. My plan had been to tell Wendy on the day her flight left, but I ended up letting her in on the secret a couple of days beforehand.

She was absolutely stunned. 'What? You've booked me flights to London and Paris . . . in three days' time?'

The giving has to be unconditional. You can't give while secretly hoping or expecting the other person will do the same.

'Yep, honey. It's an adventure for you, to go and surprise your dad! He has no idea you are coming.'

She hugged me and squealed with joy . . . Then took off to start packing.

I loved being able to surprise Wendy with something so cool, as she had supported me so much over the years. It's true that the more you give to another person, the more they give to you. The giving has to be unconditional, though. You can't give while secretly hoping or expecting the other person will do the same.

Wendy arrived at the place where her parents were staying in Paris with perfect timing, as they were just arriving as well.

She walked up to her dad and said, 'Hi, Dad!'

Her father, Brian, just stood and stared at her. He couldn't work out who she was. After a few moments, he clicked that this woman in front of him was his youngest daughter. They all had a good laugh, but it wasn't until later that Brian confessed he'd initially thought she was one of the local prostitutes he'd seen walking around. Nice one, Brian . . .

Ethan at seven years old, on his first trip with Dad to see Everest.
We're at Namche Bazaar, the gateway to the high Himalaya.

Presenting a replica yeti hand and skull to the lamas at Pangboche
monastery, to replace the ones that were stolen. The replicas were
made for us by the amazing team at Weta Workshop in Wellington.

My favourite photo of Maya from her seven-year-old
trip. She's so clearly loving life in the Himalaya.

A proud moment: pointing out Mount Everest to my daughter.

Maya with a storekeeper in Namche named Alan. One of our rules was that
if the kids wanted to buy something, they had to barter for it themselves.

Maya with the ever-welcoming security guard outside
Mike's Breakfast, a popular cafe in Kathmandu.

Taking a nap after some intense training for the 777 Project:
seven marathons on seven continents in seven days. Dylan's
feeling equally exhausted after his day at playgroup.

At Namche Bazaar, this time with seven-year-old Dylan. He was just as excited as Ethan and Maya had been.

Dylan with Robby, who came to live with our friend Palden Sherpa at Namaste Lodge after Robby's mother went missing. The two boys formed a really special friendship.

Dylan and Robby with some Sherpa friends at Khumjung
School. Sir Edmund Hillary was responsible for
building the classroom that Robby studied in.

Wendy (right) and her sister Penny making plans for
the day during our family trip to the Himalaya.

Nawang Sherpa and Ethan, all set for the next leg of our family trek to see Everest. The kids loved having Nawang and his brother Kusang with us.

Some working yaks on our friend Gurman's property pose for a photo with Ethan, Maya and Dylan.

Dylan smashing out a six during a friendly game
of cricket at Khumjung School.

It meant a lot for the whole family to be together in Nepal and the Himalaya.

Ethan soaking up the Himalaya mountain air on one of our
rest stops. Keeping kids fuelled is really important.

I'm always telling the kids that staying hydrated is critical, especially when
you're trekking at altitude. Maya seems to have absorbed the message!

The Allsop family with Lama Geshe, who's wearing
the jacket we gave him as a gift.

The scary part of the trek from Pangboche to Phortse,
with a steep drop of about a thousand metres on the left.
The kids loved it but Wendy wasn't too keen.

Another favourite photo: relaxing in the pool at
Hotel Manaslu with Maya and Ethan.

Dylan lighting butter lamps at Swayambhunath (the Monkey
Temple). This building was completely destroyed in the 2015
earthquake, only days after this photo was taken.

A stunning day at Sonam Lodge in Pangboche, which is run by our friend Gurman. Ama Dablam rises majestically in the background.

Two days before the 2015 earthquake hit, we were in the red building in the centre of this photo, drinking Cokes in the little cafe. Our seats were near the green sign.

Maya receiving a blessing from Lama Geshe before her world's highest stand-up paddleboard attempt.

A moment of celebration for us all as Maya achieves her goal.

I managed to convince Maya that her little joke—putting on an oxygen mask and sending a photo to her mum—was not such a great idea!

Ethan with members of our climbing team for his
Kilimanjaro challenge: Mndeme (left) and Salimu.

Perfecting my selfie technique with a little guidance from
Ethan. We're partway through the Kilimanjaro climb.

We made it! An obligatory photo in front of the
sign on the summit of Mount Kilimanjaro.

Not just an average game of Guess Who? . . . this one is taking
place on top of the highest mountain in Africa. Guinness World
Records are processing Ethan's claim to the record.

He did make up for this case of mistaken identity with his genuine delight over the effort Wendy had gone to in order to surprise him. She had a fantastic time in Paris, visiting plenty of museums, cafes and restaurants. It was her kind of adventure.

As I've mentioned, I know that a happy family adventure needs to include something for everyone. We all need to have things to look forward to, and we all need to be involved in what is happening. While I might love to head off climbing for a month or to go on a lengthy expedition to the North Pole, that isn't going to happen because those things are just about me. There's nothing in them for Wendy or for the kids. And, you know what? The North Pole and the mountains will still be there when our children have grown up. For now, the experience of seeing the Himalaya and visiting my Sherpa friends with my family is more than enough.

▲

The 18 months that we spent in preparation for our family adventure to Pangboche—saving the money and planning the leave from our jobs—flew by. We approached the kids' schools with our plans and they were extremely happy, as they saw it as a great educational opportunity. This time, we'd also be taking two more family members with us: Wendy's sister, Penny, and her brother, BJ.

The kids were all pros at the whole travel thing by now, but it was a bit different flying to Nepal with the whole family. For one, I didn't have to keep my eyes on the kids the whole time! We also had Nawang and his brother Kusang with us, and they are fantastic with kids. I loved that we were all going to be on this adventure together.

Landing in Kathmandu, the kids were super excited as all their own memories came flooding back. Twelve-year-old Ethan made quite a big deal about finally being allowed to swim in the Hotel Manaslu pool, and took every opportunity to tease me about the fact I'd let Dylan do it but not him!

Our first afternoon in Kathmandu was spent relaxing by the pool. Well, I say relaxing, but Wendy and Penny probably don't remember it that way. While we were sitting there, a huge monkey—one of the local macaques with a massive, bright red bum—came walking into the pool area like it owned the place. It actually had a swagger.

The others hadn't noticed it, but I was watching as the monkey wandered around a bit and came closer to our loungers, staring at us. I grabbed my phone and started filming just as the monkey ambled past, a few centimetres from Wendy and Penny. They both screamed, causing the monkey to shoot off up a nearby tree. Sadly, in the excitement of it all, I hadn't quite managed to push record on my phone!

The following morning, a shopping trip to sort out gear for everyone was on the agenda. One of my favourite places to go is a little shop called Shona's Alpine Rental. It caters for both the full-on Everest mountaineers and the less full-on family trekkers. Shona (go figure) and Andy own the shop. Shona is Sherpa and Andy is an English mountaineer. On an expedition to climb Lhotse, the world's fourth highest mountain, Andy lost a few toes, and as a result he is a good person to get advice from about staying warm at altitude.

Over the years, I've taken all of the kids there and kitted them out with everything they need for trekking. This time, we needed heaps of stuff, so we spent a few hours in the shop sorting out walking poles, day packs, bags for the porters to carry, gloves, hats and waterproof stuff sacks.

While the gear you can buy in Nepal is OK, the quality varies a lot, so you have to be a bit careful about what you buy. I recommend taking some good-quality gear with you and just using the shops in Kathmandu for extra stuff that you won't have to rely on to save your life—bags, poles, that kind of thing.

The one thing I never go to Nepal without is a good set of Icebreaker gear—especially the hats, socks and mid-layer tops. I wear it, and so do all the kids. When I climbed Everest, I wore two layers of Icebreaker (one of them an original 200-weight jumper I'd bought in 1999). That was all I had under my down suit and I was perfectly warm.

We flew to Lukla the next morning. The weather was lovely and clear once we got away from Kathmandu, and the Himalaya were out in spectacular form. The approach to Lukla was pretty normal and the landing was great, thanks to the skill of the pilots.

I was a bit surprised to see that Wendy was quite relaxed about the whole thing, since I knew how nervous she'd been about the flight. On the ground in Lukla, she was happily trying to take the whole scene in and was completely unfazed by the flight.

'Well done, babe. That wasn't so bad, eh?' I said.

She laughed and replied, 'No, it was great. I took two Valium before we left Kathmandu.'

Well, that's one way to get through the Lukla flight, I guess!

After the customary visit to see Dawa Sherpa at Paradise Lodge, where there was breakfast and hugs all around, we set off. The plan was for Nawang and Kusang to walk with us all the way to Pangboche, then Kusang would guide BJ up to Everest base camp. We were also joined by some porters to carry our gear, as lugging a heavy pack is the quickest way to wear yourself out when trekking at high altitude.

One of Wendy's biggest concerns, which not even a Valium could solve, was the state of the toilets on the trail. She had heard horror stories. A few times throughout the day she asked where the nearest toilet was. There wasn't anything really around, so I just kept stalling, hoping she could hang on until we reached a village.

One of Wendy's biggest concerns was the state of the toilets on the trail. She had heard horror stories.

In the end, she was so busting that she hissed at me, 'I've got to go NOW.'

Thanks to Nawang's diplomatic skills, a Sherpa lady agreed to let Wendy use her outhouse.

Wendy wasn't the only one holding her breath as she walked in. I was really nervous. This could make or break Wendy's trip . . .

After a couple of minutes, she came back out and announced, 'That was great! There were these leaves you put over it, and there was no smell.'

Whew. I breathed out, and thought, *I'm sure it helped that you were really busting*!

Wendy now says, 'Any toilet is a good toilet when you are busting!'

As we trekked along, a dog started following Dylan. Then, that night in Phakding, he and Maya befriended a cat, named it Puss and spent the whole evening fussing over it. Dylan is a dog and cat whisperer. He even has a way with yaks—more than once I saw a yak stop and stare at him.

We stayed at Sunrise Lodge in Phakding, which has great food and good rooms. It was particularly cold that night, but the kids knew the drill. They all slept with their socks and hats on, and I filled their Nalgene bottles with hot water to help keep them warm.

It was an early start in the morning, as we were planning to do a long day's walking. Instead of my usual night in Monjo, we only stopped there for a hot drink to prepare us for the slog up Namche hill. Yep, we were going from Phakding to Namche Bazaar in a single day.

When we reached the hill, we all climbed up and up, swishing back and forth, gaining altitude as we went. Then everyone stopped at the Everest lookout. This was Wendy's first glimpse of the mountain in real life. Even though it is away off in the distance, it is so impressive. It's almost hard to believe that you're looking at the highest point on the planet. She was mesmerised.

About an hour on and there was Namche. As you enter the village, there is a beautiful big stupa with prayer wheels all around it. The kids all started spinning the prayer wheels. They remembered that the wheels should be turned clockwise, and I was happy to see them respect this local custom. Each of the wheels contain Buddhist prayers and it's believed that each time the wheel is turned the prayer is repeated.

There were lots of Sherpa kids hanging out near the stupa. Some of them came up and started talking to Ethan, Maya and Dylan. Wendy and I hung back to watch our kids interact with the Sherpa children. Before long, Maya ran over to me and asked for some biscuits. I gave her a packet and she took them back to share with her new friends as they chatted. It was so cute.

As we climbed the steep steps up to Namaste Lodge, I could see Palden standing outside, surveying the arriving travellers, as he likes to do. It was so nice to see his friendly face, greeting us with a smile. We all piled into the lodge and sat down. I find that with trekking you often don't realise how hard you've worked until you sit down for the first time.

Palden's wife, Tsering, and Wendy hit it off immediately. They're both such warm, caring people that it was inevitable they'd be friends. That evening, our two families played cards together and talked. I think every single one of us slept well that night.

Unfortunately, Robby wasn't home, as he was down the valley doing a bit of work for someone else. Tsering's 14-year-old niece was there and her name was also Tsering. We all played cards and it got very competitive. Later, Palden entertained the kids with some more card tricks.

It was another early start the following morning, made all the easier by the fact most of us we were still on New Zealand time, so it felt like the middle of the afternoon. After a good breakfast, we headed over the hill towards Khumjung.

The climb out of Namche is all steep steps, which take about 30 minutes to climb. After a while, your body adapts and sort of says, 'Shit, I'm climbing hundreds of steps,' and stops hurting.

Slowly, slowly is the key—or, as Nawang says, 'Polepole', which sounds like 'pulley, pulley'.

I asked him about this saying as I remembered hearing

a similar one on Mount Kilimanjaro. Nawang laughed and said, 'It's Swahili—everyone says it on Kilimanjaro.'

To this day, I'm not sure how it found its way into Sherpa language!

Following the climb out of Namche is the meanest hill I've ever seen. It's basically a huge ridge that involves walking straight up for about an hour. Ethan and Dylan had both done it before, and thankfully none of the others seemed bothered by it.

There's a point on the way up the ridge when Ama Dablam comes into view for the first time. There she is, just towering out of the ground with her arms open wide, welcoming you into her heart. Seriously, the two ridges on either side of the summit really look like the mountain has her arms out. Ama Dablam means 'mother's necklace', in reference to a glacier that hangs on the face of the mountain like a necklace.

As we were walking up the track, I could hear the distinct sound of New Zealand accents. We soon found the source of the noise—a group of Year 12 and 13 students who were also on their way to Khumjung. It turned out they were doing their Duke of Edinburgh gold medal awards.

I got talking to the group leader as we walked, and we chatted about the whole guiding experience. He told me about all the health and safety issues involved with taking groups of school kids to Everest base camp. One of the things we agreed on was the importance of carrying smoke alarms with us to give to the tea-house owners along the way. There are so many open fires and candles that deaths due to smoke and fire are quite common. Smoke alarms are light to carry and the good ones last up to ten years. It's a small price to pay to save lives, I reckon.

Then our conversation turned to the risk of earthquakes in the region. I recounted my recent chat with a seismologist, who had told me he'd put two GPS-marked stakes 200 metres apart on a fault line and they had each moved 15 metres sideways in 12 years. He was concerned that the underlying fault line had moved so much without any release of tension.

Up on top of a nearby hill is Syangboche airport, into which building supplies, firewood and other goods are flown by helicopters and small aircraft. I've climbed up this way lots of times and I always enjoy making my way towards the top of the ridge. There are heaps of little paths cut by yaks and Sherpa, and fragrant juniper bushes everywhere. Every time I go there I choose a different path, much to Nawang's horror, but you can't get lost as you can always see the ridge where you are going.

It's hard to describe what it meant to me for Wendy to see those mountains. Without Wendy's support and her confidence in me, there is no way I could have climbed Everest.

Just before the top of the ridge is a very large stupa. As we crested the ridge we got the most amazing views of Ama Dablam and Everest. I enjoyed listening to everyone's gasps of delight—especially Wendy's—as they took in the scenery.

It's hard to describe what it meant to me for Wendy to see those mountains. Without Wendy's support and her confidence in me, there is no way I could have climbed Everest or done any of the other amazing things I've done in this place. I can barely believe that someone could support another person so much. She married me knowing I was an adventurer and that one day I wanted to climb Everest. She never tried to change me. She is a free spirit herself, and I like to think that my adventuring feeds her spirit in some way as well.

As we stood and took in the incredible view, we all started to get a bit cold. Time to put on another layer. Maya's hands were freezing—but that's what happens if you don't put your gloves on when Dad suggests you do. Nawang happily rubbed her little hands to warm them up and get the blood flowing again.

About 45 minutes later, we walked down to the school at Khumjung. It was closed for the weekend, but there were a few kids playing on the bone-dry, dusty soccer pitch. I had brought a cricket bat and ball with us, and soon enough my kids and some of the Sherpa children were playing cricket— to the sound of me shouting, 'No running! No running! You're at fourteen thousand feet! No running . . .' They didn't listen.

Near the school, there was a pop-up dental surgery going on, so we went over and said hello. Everyone was very friendly and the head dentist told us all about the programme. Interestingly, he said that one of the biggest issues is trekkers giving the kids sweets. Their diets contain very little sugar and they don't usually brush their teeth twice a day, as they don't always have easy access to toothpaste or even water, so the trekkers' lollies are causing cavities.

I'd been told not to bring sweets before I first came to Nepal, but I wanted to bring some treats for the kids. The first year, I brought balloons. The first young Sherpa boy I gave one to looked a bit confused, so I blew up another balloon to show him what to do. He looked delighted and put the balloon to his lips, but instead of blowing he inhaled sharply. The balloon got sucked back into his mouth and he started making a choking noise. I panicked and went to grab him just as he coughed it up. It was only a split second, but I got a huge shock. Non-inflated balloons: fail.

Then I tried blowing up the balloons before I gave them to the kids. As I walked away, I heard a pop, followed by crying. Inflated balloons: fail.

The following year, I took marbles with me. I met some young kids and showed them how to play, and we had a cool little game. Then one child picked up a marble and put it in his mouth. His mother grabbed him and tried to get it out of his mouth, but he refused to spit it out. She tipped him upside down and started slapping his back. Eventually, he gave up the marble after much screaming and crying. Marbles: fail.

Now I take pens, pencils and little stickers. Kids the world over love getting a little sticker put on their hand.

CHAPTER 11

KHUMJUNG AND THE YETI

After saying goodbye to the dentist, we had some lunch at a little tea house. I asked Ethan if he wanted another milkshake, but he didn't seem keen! Instead, we had Rara noodle soup made with instant noodles and washed down with sweet milk tea. There wasn't much chance of setting sick from any of that.

A few tourists walk over from Namche for the day to visit the school and a few might stay the night, but Khumjung is mostly a traditional Sherpa farming village. One farmer explained it to me this way: 'Namche people have lots of money and no potatoes. Khumjung people have no money and lots of potatoes.'

One place we were all keen to visit was the local monastery in Khumjung, which had a yeti skull (not a replica like the one I had brought to Pangboche!). We spoke to the caretaker monk, asked to see the skull and paid him a few rupees to show it to us. The skull is locked in a glass box. Standing about 30 centimetres high, it is cone shaped and has dark brownish-ginger and black hair attached to it. It looks like leather. When Sir Edmund Hillary led his yeti-finding expedition in the 1960s, his team was allowed to take it away and examine it. They concluded that it was a fake. However, back then they had limited technology with which to make that decision. With the advanced DNA testing available now, it would be very interesting to see which animal the skull has come from.

The kids all gathered around the glass case, asking lots of questions. 'Is it real, Dad? Is it like the one Weta Workshop made for you? Come on, Dad. Do yetis really exist?'

I wanted to keep the mystery alive as long as possible, so I deflected their 'Is it real?' questions.

On our way back to Namche, which was about a three-hour walk, the clouds rolled in. It got really cold as we headed back over the ridge, and I was very happy to have Nawang with us. He fussed over the kids, zipped up their tops and helped them to put on their jackets.

All of us had 'buffs' with us. These are tubes of material that can be worn heaps of different ways. A good Sherpa trick is to put the buff around your neck then pull the bottom of it around and up over your ears and the back of your head, then put your hat on top of it. Super warm.

By the time we got back to Palden's, we were all a little tired so were happy to settle in for a night that consisted of

Tsering's famous chilli chicken, sweet milk tea and games of cards and chess.

The following day, we pushed further on up the valley, stopping for the night to see Tashi at Kyangjuma. Her dog Maya had just had puppies, which the kids thought was just fantastic. Maya found it funny that the dog had the same name as her, and she begged me to take a puppy home with us. Wendy was really happy to find that the rooms had en suite toilets!

After dinner at Tashi's house, we sat down with a group of visiting monks and lamas who were on their way to Kathmandu. We all watched the Brad Pitt movie *Seven Years in Tibet*. It was a slightly surreal experience, but it was interesting to see the monks' reactions to the movie.

The kids were transfixed as there were Tibetan monks in the movie who looked just like the ones sitting right there watching it with them. They couldn't understand why China invaded Tibet, and they all found the battle scenes very sad. I think Maya took it to heart the most as she talked about it a lot, and to this day it is one of her favourite movies.

There was an easy start to trekking the following morning, as we walked down to the valley floor all the way to the banks of the Dudh Koshi river. I knew we had a big climb coming up in the form of the Tengboche hill, which is just as big as the climb up to Namche if not bigger. It was time to bring out the snacks for morning tea. I always carry nuts, dried fruit and popcorn, and this time I had some small packets of beef jerky as well. This particular morning, the kids all got some popcorn. It's amazing stuff when trekking with kids, as it gives them energy without the sugar rush. I mean, the post-chocolate sugar rush is fine; it's just that the crash afterwards is terrible. That's why I always try to stay away from anything with heaps of sugar in it while we're trekking, with the exception of cups of hot chocolate at the tea houses along the way. Another bonus of eating popcorn is that the kids drink heaps of water, which is important at altitude.

We took our time as we climbed Tengboche hill. It was hard going and we were all stopping a lot to catch our breath. I was a little bit worried about the time. We didn't get to the top of the hill until 2.30pm, and I wanted to spend a while exploring the local monastery, but we still had another few hours' trekking before we'd make it to Pangboche. To make matters worse, at Tengboche the weather started to change. The clouds rolled in and the temperature dropped.

Tengboche Monastery is an amazing sight, and totally worth the time to explore. The original building was destroyed by an earthquake in 1934, then its replacement burned to the ground in 1989. Thankfully, two trekkers ran into the burning building and saved a lot of the prayer books, mantra cards and other important artefacts.

The monastery was rebuilt a second time thanks to the work of volunteers and an international fundraising effort, which included support from Sir Edmund Hillary. I remember seeing a film about Sir Ed that showed him being welcomed into the new monastery. In typical Sir Ed fashion, he turned to his mate and said, 'Wow, this place is huge. I didn't think we were building a cathedral!'

The monastery is beautiful. We walked up the magnificent steps inside to see a rock with two distinct footprints in it. The local people believe the first lama to come to the area flew across the Himalaya from Tibet and landed right on that spot, leaving his footprints.

He then settled here and lived a peaceful life, and the yeti even came down from the mountains and helped him farm his crops. Apparently, they worked together for a long time before something happened that caused the yeti to go back into the mountains, where they now only look down on the monastery from high above.

There was this beautiful sound coming through the walls, a sound lost in time. The kids' eyes were wide open; they had never heard anything like it.

In the main prayer chamber, the lamas and monks were all chanting their mantras. There was this beautiful sound coming through the walls, a sound lost in time. The kids' eyes were wide open; they had never heard anything like it.

Everyone was a little nervous as they gathered around me for a little briefing before going into the main body of the monastery. 'Take off your shoes, turn off your phones, and don't get your cameras out. Please be very respectful as it is such a privilege for us to see these monks and lamas performing their daily practice.' I then gave each of the kids some money.

A monk pulled back a tall curtain and gently ushered us in. We each put a small donation into the box and then tip-toed around the outside of the room. It was so beautifully decorated. Maya pointed to one of the paintings and whispered in my ear, 'Dad, there's Green Tara! Look.' That was the goddess in the name Lama Geshe had given her.

We all sat down on the floor and crossed our legs. I closed my eyes and listened to this deep, ancient chanting that seemed to come from another world. Then I opened one eye and looked at the kids. All three of them were sitting there with their eyes closed as well.

We stayed for about 15 minutes, then quietly made our way back outside. We were all really moved by the experience, especially Wendy. She looked at me and her expression of joy said it all.

My mind soon jolted back to reality. It was getting late and we still had three hours' hard walking to get to Pangboche. As we walked down into a beautiful rhododendron forest, I pulled Nawang aside and told him that I was worried we wouldn't get there before dark and it would turn into what mountaineers call an 'epic': an unexpectedly huge day. Now, having an epic isn't always bad, but I reckon it's best to avoid them if you can. I'm sure we would have been fine doing the last bit of the walk in the dark, but this was supposed to be a fun adventure, not an intrepid one.

Nawang told me not to worry. 'I know a tea house to stay in. It's run by my family . . .' It is so good having a friend like him.

About an hour later, we arrived at the tea house and got some rooms for the night. It was nice and warm, and the rooms were good, but the toilets were terrible. It looked like a lot of people had been very sick when using them . . . Out came the hand-sanitiser bottles and a reminder lecture about the importance of clean hands and not putting your fingers anywhere near your mouth. My last words were, 'No one wants diarrhoea.'

Then Dylan piped up, 'Yeah, Dad, no one wants bum wees!' I think he summed that up better than I ever could.

Gastrointestinal issues are not uncommon in Nepal, but the bugs are all bacterial up at altitude, so getting the right antibiotics can make all the difference. The worst thing you can do is take anti-diarrhoea medication as it just blocks you up and stops the bugs from working their way out of your system.

While we waited for dinner, we sat around talking and

playing chess. Then I realised that I didn't know where Dylan was. I looked everywhere for him. He wasn't in his room or in the toilet. He hadn't come back to the dining area. It was dark outside and I was starting to panic a little bit. He was only eight, after all.

Nawang soon put my mind at ease. He'd seen Dylan talking to one of the old Sherpa women and she had taken him to her house next door to feed him. I found him sitting in the kitchen with three Sherpa women all fussing over him. It was really dark and they were cooking dinner for some workers, guides and porters over a wood-fired stove. Dylan was perfectly relaxed, soaking up the somewhat smoky atmosphere! He was showing one of the Sherpa women one of Palden's card tricks and they were all laughing away. Nawang and I stayed with him for a while, then we all went back over to the main lodge.

As the temperature plummeted, I filled everyone's Nalgene bottles with hot water. Not only did they have hot-water bottles to keep them warm now, they'd have cool water to drink in the morning. Up the Everest valley, boiled water is my little secret for a healthy tummy.

We were woken by Maya running into our room in the morning. 'Dad! Dad! Look out the window!'

There was about half a metre of fresh snow blanketing the whole area and it was still falling heavily.

The kids and I got dressed fast, and went outside to play in the snow. Maya soon started building a snowman with a bit of help from Dylan. Ethan was inside playing chess and staying warm. It was really dry snow so I wasn't too worried about them getting wet. That would have been a disaster as we had limited changes of clothes, and nothing dries until night-time when the Sherpa light their fires.

There were a few tents in the field we were in, and I stood there thinking about how cool it must have been to be in one of them while it snowed. Next thing, the tent was unzipped and a head popped out. It was Dr Raj, who had been with an army team at base camp on Everest when I'd been there. We had a good catch-up, and it was great to be able to introduce him to my kids.

Back at the tea house, as we all got ready to leave, I did my best not to let on that I was worried about the walk ahead of us. I was nervous that the snow would make our trek even longer, and that it would be freezing and icy.

At one point, the path had been eroded by a huge slip. The drop down was about 60 metres, and the path was covered with ice. Penny stopped to take a picture right at the worst spot, and all I could see was the kids trying to walk around her on this narrow, icy bit of path. One slip and that'd be it: gone! I was really stressed, but tried not to show it as I asked Penny not to stop there.

I mustn't have tried hard enough, because moments later Wendy came over and told me off for snapping at Penny and upsetting her. My stress level was about a ten, I must admit. I apologised to Penny and explained I was worried about one of the kids slipping. Along with steep, icy slopes, I was also very worried about yaks.

Nawang, on the other hand, was worried about the kids getting snow-blind. I've never seen him that worried. He called Gurman Sherpa at Pangboche and asked him to bring some sunglasses for the kids. Gurman arrived about 40 minutes later with three pairs of sunglasses, then walked back to the village with us.

The main Pangboche bridge had collapsed some time before and was a huge mess of tangled steel and wire. The locals built another bridge a bit further up the river. It looked stunning under its blanket of snow.

After crossing the new bridge, it was back to climbing. I got a bit of a kick as we walked past the stupa that I'd organised all the cement for and helped to paint with the second Everest base camp team. It was such an honour to walk past a monument that has such significance to the people of Pangboche and quietly know that my friends and I helped rebuild it.

As we walked up the hill, I saw my worst fear coming straight towards us: a 15-strong yak train.

It's a very steep climb up into Pangboche from the stupa, and it takes about 20 minutes. As we walked up the hill, I saw my worst fear coming straight towards us: a 15-strong yak train. My head almost exploded with fear. *What if a yak falls on one of the kids? Or slips on the ice and squashes one of the kids? What if a yak gets mad and sticks its horn into one of the kids?* The possibilities seemed gruesomely endless.

I remembered the yak that came flying at Ethan in Namche when he was seven—it had nearly taken him out, and there hadn't been any snow or ice then. I also thought of Ang Nuru's good friend who was killed when he was gored by a yak horn.

I looked up to see that Nawang and Gurman had taken Maya and Ethan off the track and up the bank a little bit. Dylan and I tucked ourselves into a small alcove of rock a couple of metres from the path. From our relatively safe spots, we watched as the yaks piled past with their beautiful bells ringing away in the clear air. Dylan was asking loads of questions about them. 'How heavy are their packs, Dad? How far do you think they're going?'

All that panic was for nothing in the end. It's funny how irrational you can get when you think about your kids getting hurt.

The three kids all carried on up the track with Nawang, Gurman and Kusang keeping a close eye on them. You can't get safer than that in the Himalaya! This left Wendy and me to walk into Pangboche together. The snow was falling and we were holding hands as I explained what this tiny village meant to me. I pointed out the homes of the Sherpa I knew. Wendy had heard so much about Pangboche and I was excited to finally be showing it to her. It looked so beautiful with the snow falling.

We arrived at Sonam Lodge, which is Gurman's place and a home for my soul. I had spent ten days there in 2007 waiting for a weather window so I could climb Everest. We had played many games of cards and visited the monastery numerous times as I tried not to think about what was going to happen in the following weeks.

Sonam Lodge has an awesome dining room with a fire right in the middle. Gurman had the fire stoked to the maximum. We all took off a few layers of clothes and our gloves, and crowded around the fire.

Gurman and his wife brought us cups of sweet tea, soup and plates of homemade chips. The kids fitted in straight away, and I could tell that they felt right at home. Ethan started playing chess with Gurman's son. They played for hours. Maya and Dylan had a few card games and then ran around the place, sometimes shovelling snow, sometimes throwing it, playing just like it was their home.

As the temperature dropped that night, we all gathered around and I told a few stories about the yeti. Gurman's son looked at me and said, 'Mike, this creature does not exist. It is all legend and mystery.'

After my talk, Maya started asking if we could go yeti hunting. I brushed her off and changed the subject, as the last thing I felt like doing was trekking uphill in the freezing cold. But by 8pm, she'd convinced me that yeti hunting had to be done.

It was probably a few degrees below freezing, so Maya and I rugged up and set off up the hill in the pitch dark. Our head torches lit the path in front of us. As we got higher, I could feel Maya's hand squeezing mine harder and harder. To tell the truth, I was a little scared myself.

We stopped and looked at the stars, which are super bright as there is very little light pollution at that altitude. A couple of hundred metres below us we could see the lights of the lodge. It was very dark and very quiet.

Maya sat down and said, 'OK, Dad. Let's look for yeti.'

'All right,' I said. 'You face that way, and I'll watch behind us as yeti normally attack from behind.'

Instantly she said, 'That's enough yeti hunting, Dad. Let's go back.'

She stood up, grabbed my hand and we walked back down the hill. That little trek in the dark was enough to completely sate Maya's yeti-hunting desires!

CHAPTER 12

AMA DABLAM

I woke up early and pulled back the curtain, and there was Ama Dablam looking down on me, her arms wide open. There is no other mountain like it in the world. Upon seeing the mountain for the first time, Sir Edmund Hillary described it as unclimbable, but it was first successfully summited by a team of four climbers that included Kiwis Mike Gill and Wally Romanes.

I could hear the kids outside helping Gurman feed his yaks. I'm usually a bit nervous about them being around yaks, but a couple of Gurman's ones were really tame. One was especially chilled out. He was huge and had a big white head, so his nickname was Whitehead. The kids stroked his mane, patted his side and touched his horns, and he just stood there happily eating. Whitehead was a lovely yak—

unlike most of the others, which were very feisty. Even Gurman was cautious around them when they were feeding.

That day was very important as I was taking the whole family to see Lama Geshe, and Nawang was coming with us to translate. I was a bit worried I would lose it and start crying when I saw the lama. He has a very special aura about him, and you feel you are in the presence of greatness when you are near him.

We slowly walked up the hill to his house, passing the Pangboche Monastery on the way. Everyone spun the prayer wheels as we walked around the building. Tears were already welling in my eyes and I had to try to hold them off.

We entered Lama Geshe's home, and his daughter, Tashi, told us he wasn't that well so we could only stay for about 20 minutes. Then we were taken to the main room, where he was sitting in the corner. He had a big smile on his face and I'm pretty sure he recognised me. Nawang introduced me and, as I walked towards the lama with my head bowed low out of respect, tears flowed down my cheeks. I handed him my white silk prayer scarf with a small donation rolled inside it. He put a thin cotton necklace around my neck, said a Buddhist prayer and gently pulled my head towards his until our foreheads touched.

I looked up and felt a sense of peace. I gave him a big smile. Then I sat there and watched each of my children come into the room, heads bowed. Each of them was very respectful. They had heard me speak about Lama Geshe all their lives, and I could sense that meeting him was a big deal for them too.

Dylan was first and Nawang said his Tibetan name, Dalha.

Lama Geshe asked Tashi to confirm the name again. He took a second look at Dylan and in his deep voice repeated 'Dalha', then let out a deep chuckle.

Maya was next. There was a bit of discussion and the name 'Maya' was repeated several times as Lama Geshe looked back and forth between Nawang and my daughter. Then he stopped, looked straight at her and said, 'Namkha Dolma.'

Then it was Ethan's turn. Lama Geshe said something to Ethan in Tibetan and Ethan replied 'Tsering Dorje' with a big smile.

Wendy came into the room next. When Lama Geshe was told her name, he said 'Windy' very loudly and chuckled. Wendy had a beautiful smile as she bowed in front of him.

I have received a few of Lama Geshe's blessings over the years and each and every one has been special. This one was the most special of them all.

We all sat down and Lama Geshe's wife brought us sweet tea. Nawang spoke a little and then it was time for Lama Geshe's formal blessing.

I have received a few of Lama Geshe's blessings over the years and each and every one has been special. This one was the most special of them all, as I watched my kids and Wendy all sitting there in front of him.

After Lama Geshe finished his blessing, we presented him with a gift. When I had seen him 18 months earlier, I had asked if there was anything I could do to help him. I mentioned that his roof was looking a bit old and asked if he would like help replacing it. He looked at me and smiled, then spoke in Tibetan. Tashi translated: 'My father would like a new down jacket, size XL.'

So it was a pretty neat moment as the kids all lined up to give him his new jacket. It had been specially made for him by Shona back in Kathmandu. It was a very specific shade of red and it couldn't have any black on it. Buddhist monks do not wear black.

Lama Geshe made a fuss of the kids and asked them to put the jacket on him. It took a little time as he shuffled around speaking to the kids in Tibetan. I just sat there with a huge smile on my face, watching them help him with his jacket. It fitted perfectly and he looked chuffed.

He then pointed for the kids to sit down and there was lots of discussion as he started making these small square necklaces. The necklaces were made out of folded paper that had prayers written on them. Inside each of them was blessed rice, a special bead from a sacred mountain and a Himalayan eagle feather. Both Nawang and Tashi said that this was a great privilege. He presented each of us with these very special necklaces and told us that we must either have them with us or leave them in our house to protect ourselves and our home.

All up, we spent about 90 minutes with Lama Geshe and we all left feeling very happy. As we walked back to Sonam Lodge, Wendy and I held hands while the kids skipped ahead of us with Nawang.

Wendy looked at me and said, 'That was so powerful. It's hard to describe the feeling.' I knew exactly what she meant.

The next morning we were due to set off on the four-hour walk to Phortse village. As we packed, the weather started to turn bad. I asked Nawang and Gurman what they thought, and both of them said it would be OK, but I had an uneasy feeling in my stomach. The weather looked different from anything I'd seen before. Usually, the storms roll up the valley, starting down low and building up. This one looked more like a very dark wall. I decided to stay put for an hour to see what would happen.

The storm hit an hour later and it snowed so heavily that if we'd been trekking in it we would have had to turn around and come back. Decision made. We stayed another night, ate, played cards, fed the yaks and relaxed.

The kids played in the snow, shovelled it, threw it at each other, and their smiles said it all. Here, there was no Wi-Fi, no phones, no computer games, and they couldn't have been happier.

The following day dawned sunny and fine. Before we left, the kids played cricket with Gurman and Nawang and a few other Sherpa. It was hilarious seeing some of these Sherpa with a cricket bat for the first time, hitting the ball and running. There was one small issue that Kiwi cricketers never have to deal with—you had to be careful when the ball landed by a yak!

As we said goodbye, Gurman put white silk scarfs around our necks and gave the kids a bottle of Sprite each. We'd had such an awesome three nights with him, and it was sad to be leaving.

▲

The trek to Phortse is one of the most spectacular routes in the Khumbu Valley—and by spectacular I mean there are huge drops off the side of the track. I knew Wendy was going to freak out.

As we trekked along, two beautiful Himalayan golden eagles circled above us, which distracted Wendy for a little while. Then we got to a point where the track climbs very steeply, with a rock face on the right going up and a drop on the left of about a thousand metres, almost straight down to the river. If you fell off, there would be no stopping until you hit the bottom.

The track consisted of stone steps only 30 centimetres wide in places. The kids thought it was great, but Wendy was white with fear and shaking! I positioned a Sherpa between each kid and sent Wendy off first.

If you fell off, there would be no stopping until you hit the bottom. The kids thought it was great, but Wendy was white with fear and shaking!

She turned around a few times and tried to talk to me. I told her to concentrate on her steps and that the kids would be fine. She leaned into the rock face and got up the path, no problem. I followed with my heart in my mouth. I was very glad we weren't doing it in a snow storm.

As we descended into the little village of Phortse, there were yaks grazing everywhere. The track was a bit muddy and I slipped. It felt like it happened in slow motion. Up I went in the air, both feet out in front of me, then I landed flat on my back. Boom! Wet, sticky clay mud all over me . . . The kids thought it was hilarious and teased me endlessly.

We stayed with a Sherpa called Pemba at his parents' tea house. That evening, I took Maya out for a little walk, just the two of us, to watch the sunset. It was pretty spectacular seeing the sun go down over the mountains. I sat there thinking how magic it was and how lucky we were.

When Maya and I walked back to the tea house, the sun had disappeared behind the Himalaya and the sky was changing colour to beautiful pinks and dark blues. The temperature dropped significantly and when you inhaled the cold bit into your nostrils. Combined with the sunset, it felt like all of my senses were on fire. It was amazing.

I looked at Maya's happy face and thought about how grateful I was for her and the other two kids in my life. But, most of all, I felt so grateful to have Wendy there with me. Her being part of this adventure was amazing, but more importantly she was just loving it. At that moment my eyes filled with tears and I had a huge smile on my face. I will never forget it.

▲

After a good sleep, we woke to a beautiful morning and were treated to a breakfast of porridge, fresh eggs and homemade bread. As we said goodbye to Pemba's parents, the sounds of the working Sherpa village were all around us. The yaks were calling for their calves, and the Sherpa were going about their daily work. We were the only tourists in Phortse as it's off the main trekking trail. It's a really lovely village so we felt quite lucky to be the only visitors.

Our trek for the day would take us all the way down to the river at the bottom of the valley, then we had a huge climb back up to Namche. It would take about eight hours, going nice and slowly with the kids and making plenty of stops along the way, including tea breaks and lunch breaks in which we did our best to get the kids to eat as much as possible.

As we climbed up the massive hill towards Namche, the kids didn't really moan, but they did ask me the same question in different ways. 'How long to the top, Dad? How far to go, Dad? Are we nearly there, Dad?'

It didn't matter if we were two hours away or 30 minutes away, the answer was the same. 'About ten minutes to go.' It drove the kids nuts.

As we approached the top of the hill, it started to snow. We stopped at the little tea house there and ordered cups of tea and hot chocolate and something to eat. Everyone was pretty tired, but there wasn't any moaning at all. I think the kids knew that it was all downhill from there to Namche— even it if was going to take us three hours!

Then, out of the blue, BJ and Kusang walked in. They had left Everest base camp the previous week and had been trying to catch up with us. Wendy let out a little shriek and jumped up from the table to hug BJ, as did Penny and all the kids. It was so nice to see him, as we hadn't had contact with him for a few days. Now we were a team again.

CHAPTER 13

HEADING FOR HOME

We all rolled into Namche in really good form. No one was exhausted or anything. Palden was there, waiting to welcome us. Tsering fussed over the kids and helped them take off some of their snow-covered gear. While they drank hot chocolate, Palden handed me an Everest beer.

By now, Namche felt like a home away from home for the Allsops. The kids knew all the tiny little shops and, as soon as they could, took off to explore them. The only thing I asked was that they all stick together and not to go too far.

Even though they were only twelve, ten and eight, they were all right into haggling for souvenirs. After each purchase, they'd run back to the lodge and tell us stories of what had happened. 'The Sherpa lady said this, so I said . . .'

We could see the excitement on their faces. It was a huge adventure for them, and it was great to see them so happy.

Those smiles were replaced with a few tears the next morning as we left for Phakding. We all hugged Palden and Tsering goodbye and sadly walked out of Namche and back down the hill, accompanied by Nawang and Kusang. It was especially sad for Dylan, as Robby hadn't made it back from down the valley in time to see him.

Back at the river, we all crossed the massive swing bridge. Wendy stared straight ahead the whole way, almost as if she had blinkers on. I could tell she hated these bridges. The kids, meanwhile, absolutely loved it—they chatted away happily as they walked across it, oblivious to the 150-metre drop just below their feet.

After a night in Phakding, where the kids were happy to see their old friend Puss the cat, we had our last day's walking—about 15 kilometres back to Lukla.

Just before we got to Lukla, I gathered the kids together and asked them to walk past me slowly and smile at the camera so I could film them walking into the town. I went ahead of them a wee bit and waited for them to come around the corner. The next thing I knew, they all came flying up the hill towards me at huge speed, racing each other. There was no slow walk or smile—just a lot of huffing, puffing and laughter. This was followed by a few high-fives and slaps on the back once they got well past me!

That night we stayed with Dawa Sherpa at Paradise Lodge. She was so pleased to see the kids and fussed over them a lot. We still had a few hours until dinner so we went into town for cake and coffee and, of course, more souvenir shopping for the kids.

After that, the kids and I headed over to the helicopter pad at the airport to watch the choppers coming and going. We recognised one of the pilots who'd just come in to land — it was my friend Jason, who the kids had met in Kathmandu. He's a longline specialist, which means he flies the chopper while another crew member dangles from it on a long rope and rescues people off mountains. It's an incredibly skilled and quite dangerous job, and he's saved many lives.

Jason was showing the kids his helicopter when his phone rang. His demeanour changed slightly and I heard him taking the details of an emergency up the valley. As he continued to speak on the phone, there was movement around us as the doors were quickly taken off a helicopter and fuel containers were filled, ready for the impending rescue mission. I glanced up the valley; the weather didn't look very good.

Jason finished his call and told me that there was someone who needed to be evacuated from Pherichie, as they were suffering from severe altitude sickness. However, Jason had made the difficult decision that the weather was not good enough for him to fly up there. It must have been a pretty hard call for him to make, knowing someone's life was in the balance, but I completely understood it. The kids were unaware of all this.

Jason headed back to his office while the kids and I stayed around observing the action. As we were standing there watching another chopper get pre-flight checks done, the pilot came over and said he'd just been called out to do a rescue from Pherichie. He asked me what the weather was like. It was a bit odd, given I was just a random guy standing there. Maybe I looked like a chopper pilot? I don't know.

I told him that I'd heard it wasn't very good and that

Jason wasn't willing to risk making the flight. The pilot seemed a bit nervous, but went back to his chopper and a few minutes later he took off. Apparently, the travel insurance company had called around all the helicopter companies until they found one that was willing to risk taking the flight. I never found out what happened.

After a dinner of Dawa Sherpa's famous sizzling chicken, we all snuck out to go to the pub. Yes, I know we're grown-ups, but Dawa doesn't really like it when her guests go out on the town in Lukla. I guess it's understandable, having seen a few members of trekking teams get a bit loose celebrating at the local Irish bar. (Yep, there is an Irish bar in Lukla. In fact, there is even one in Namche!)

With the kids in tow, we headed to the pub. The bar is underground and as we walked down the stairs we could see all the nightclub lights flashing away—yet we were the only ones there. The kids thought it was so cool having the dancefloor to themselves, and soon enough we were all up there dancing with them. It was the perfect way to spend our last night in Lukla.

We were up early to catch the first flight out to Kathmandu the following morning. After a quick breakfast, we walked over to the airport terminal. On the way, we saw Jason walking across the runway. He was off to work, rescuing someone, so we waved and shouted hello as he went.

As usual, the airport terminal was quite chaotic. Once we'd checked our bags in and had them and ourselves weighed, we had to take the bags over to a military policeman. He opened them all and had a good rifle around inside. With each one, he'd go through the same performance: he'd pull out random bits of gear and ask, 'What is it?'

'That's my torch. That's my SteriPEN. That's my phone.' And so it went, until he gave up and sent us on to get frisked.

The women and girls are frisked by a policewoman, and the boys and men get the treatment from a policeman. The frisking ranges from a light single touch to a very rigorous all-over rubdown. I've even had a good pat on my private bits . . . The type of treatment you get is always a surprise. This time it was just a light pat of my arms and knees— much to my relief.

It was one of those little moments in life when I stopped and thought, *This is so cool for these kids. What an adventure!*

Suddenly a siren sounded—but no one else seemed bothered by it. I asked a couple of people what it meant and got different answers each time. One said that it meant the first aircraft for the day had left Kathmandu; another told me that it meant there was a plane on the approach. I think it just signalled that the airport was open for the day, and was a warning that people should probably stop walking on the runway.

Before long, plane after plane began to arrive. There was even more activity as passengers and freight were offloaded and a separate group of passengers and freight was loaded on—all while each plane had one engine running. This reduces the number of cycles on the engines and saves money, which is not exactly safe when loading passengers.

I was walking behind Dylan out towards the plane, and he turned back to me and gave me this huge smile. He looked so happy, his eyes wide open, excited about the day ahead. It was one of those little moments in life when I stopped and thought, *This is so cool for these kids. What an adventure!*

As we crossed the tarmac towards our plane, there were four or five police officers all blowing their whistles and shouting at people, telling them not to stop, to do this, to do that . . . The noise was deafening.

Once on board, I looked around to make sure the kids were there and had their seat belts on. Before I'd even had time to think, the other engine had been fired up and we were taxiing towards the runway, about to make the most dangerous take-off in the world.

There was no mucking around as the pilot taxied quickly into place. The brakes were then jolted on while the pilots applied full power in order to check the engine. The aircraft vibrated noisily as it strained on its brakes—and then we were away.

We were all pushed back into our seats as the aircraft lurched forward, accelerating down the sloped runway— there was no way we'd be able to stop if anything was wrong now. It would be straight down the cliff at the end of the runway and into the river below.

The aircraft screamed down the runway right to the very end, then with a slight rotation the earth fell away beneath our wheels and we were flying. This is one take-off that definitely gets the adrenaline pumping. Wendy wore a nervous smile; I don't think she'd taken a Valium this time!

The kids' faces were all glued to the windows, looking outside. Someone let out a 'Wow!' as we took off and the earth fell away from the plane.

As we got closer to Kathmandu, the clear air began to give way to the haze of smoke that hangs over the city. As we got lower, the visibility got worse, and while we could still see the ground we couldn't see anything off in the distance. The kids were still just as intrigued, studying the landscape intently and asking the odd question.

As the runway appeared below us, and the light thud of the plane landing was followed by the squeak of the wheels hitting the ground, I said a little thank you. I always do this after a flight in or out of Lukla. I'm not sure who I'm thanking. The universe, I guess.

Arriving back at Hotel Manaslu after being in the mountains was lovely as there were familiar, friendly faces to welcome us. We got our key, dumped our bags, had showers and headed off to a cafe called Mike's Breakfast.

This place is a bit of an institution in Kathmandu. On arrival there, we were welcomed by the uniformed guard who stands outside. He's been there every time I've visited since 2005, but I have no idea just how long he has worked there. Anyway, he gave us a huge, exaggerated salute and ushered us into the restaurant.

The restaurant's beautiful terracotta-tiled garden had lots of nooks and crannies for the kids to explore. There was also an aviary in the corner that was home to two peacocks: one male and one female. Every time I go to Mike's Breakfast, the female seems annoyed at the male, as he continuously tries to impress her by extending his tail feathers into that classic half-circle peacock display. The waiter gave the kids some food for the peacocks, and I'm still not sure how no one lost a finger let alone any skin!

After a few lazy hours of chatting and laughing over coffees, smoothies and breakfast, we piled into a taxi and went back to the hotel. The kids spent about three minutes in their room before—boom!—everyone was in the pool. My favourite memory of that day is captured in a photo of me, Maya and Ethan in the pool: I have an Everest beer on the poolside and the two kids are hanging off my shoulder with huge smiles on their faces. We're all really relaxed, and I can see that everyone is loving life, the adventure and the moment we are in. I wish we could live like that every day.

That night, we had dinner at a Nepalese restaurant where, as well as traditional food, they had some local dancers perform. After two weeks in the mountains eating mainly veges, the last thing I felt like eating was vegetable curry, but the atmosphere was great and the dancers were amazing to watch.

Leaving the restaurant was a real shock to our senses. Over the past couple of weeks, we'd got used to the space and quiet of the high-altitude villages and suddenly here we were in the big city. Kathmandu comes to life at night—there are lights everywhere, the noise is awesome, there are heaps of cars and motorbikes beeping and revving, and then there's the smell of delicious food and the other smells that aren't so delicious. It is a big, colourful, noisy, vibrant overload, which we joined in as our rickshaws raced back to the hotel.

On our last full day in Nepal, we took a taxi over to Swayambhunath, which is known to foreigners as the Monkey Temple on account of the sacred monkeys that live in its north-western grounds.

By now, the whole family knew the taxi drivers at the local cab rank by name. One of the drivers, Ram, rounded up his mate and off we went across town in two tiny taxis with no seat belts, beeping the horn the whole way!

When we arrived at the temple, there were heaps of people there. As we paid our entry fee, I made sure we got a huge pile of one-rupee coins, which we then divided between us and threw into the wishing-well fountain. The kids all competed to get one to land on the statue in the middle of the fountain. Everyone was on a high.

We bought some popcorn to feed the monkeys, but I was a little wary as I'd had a close encounter with a greedy monkey on an earlier visit to the temple—it had run up and grabbed the whole bag of popcorn out of my hand. This time, I made sure that we all threw the popcorn to the monkeys before they had a chance to get near us.

The kids took it in turns to light the lamps, and as each of them did so I could see them reflecting to themselves quietly.

In one of the shrines, I bought a whole lot of butter lamps, which are used in religious practices and meditation (the name comes from the fact that the lamps traditionally burn yak butter). The kids took it in turns to light the lamps, and as each of them did so I could see them reflecting to themselves quietly. I didn't ask them what they were thinking about; I didn't need to, because I could see it on their faces. They knew that they were lighting the butter lamps as a sign of respect for the Hindu culture and they took it seriously.

One of the monkeys was sitting on a really cool part of the temple, and I wanted to get a photograph of it. I took out my GoPro camera, put it on the end of an extendable pole and proceeded to push it in the monkey's direction. The monkey got a bit restless and started to move, then looked directly at me. At the same time, a voice from behind me said, 'I wouldn't do that if I were you.'

I put my camera down straight away and asked why.

'That is how they catch the sick monkeys here. That one will get frightened and run down your pole and attack you.'

Well, that was a lucky escape!

The guy who gave me that face-saving tip was a guide at the temple, and he asked if he could show us around. He was a university student who worked as a guide to earn a little extra money. There are big advantages to having a local guide when you're in Nepal. First, they show you things you would never see or understand on your own, and second, having a guide stops all of the other guides from asking to be your guide!

He showed us around and answered all the kids' questions. 'What does that statue mean? Why are there so many butter lamps? Who lived in that temple?'

We went up a rickety old stairway, which opened out onto a little rooftop cafe. The kids drank Cokes and listened to our guide talk about his life in Kathmandu. Finally, we headed back to the hotel to pack. It was time to go home.

Nawang and his family came to the hotel to say goodbye the next morning. They gave us all beautiful silk khata scarves for luck. Then it was time to face the usual chaos at the airport.

Once on board the plane, Ethan spotted all our bags sitting on the tarmac. He joked about how good it would be if they all got offloaded and we were given compensation. The bags sat there, and each time someone went near them we all held our breath, just in case. Eventually the luggage got moved closer to the aircraft and, right at the last minute, it was loaded into the hold. No extra holiday cash for the Allsop kids this time!

As we took off, I looked down at Kathmandu and thought about what a wonderfully exciting, friendly city it was. I couldn't wait to come back.

CHAPTER 14
THE BIG ONE

Arriving back in Singapore from Kathmandu was quite something. We'd gone from one of the poorest cities in the world to one of the richest. I took a bit of time to adapt, but it didn't seem to faze the kids at all. They happily took in all the sights and sounds as they went. I don't think it mattered to them what city they were in.

On our first full day in Singapore, we went out for a bit of a wander and were on our way back to the hotel at about 2.30 in the afternoon when my phone started to blow up with text messages. I didn't think much of it at first, but when I got back to the hotel I checked the first of the messages. It was weird. It just said, 'WHERE ARE YOU?'

When I read the next message, which was from my friend Ed Overy, my heart just sank. 'There's been a huge earthquake in Kathmandu. I hope you're OK.'

Ed worked for KiwiRail and I knew that he dealt with emergency alerts as part of his job. This must be huge. I felt sick.

Someone turned on the TV. A magnitude 8 earthquake had struck Kathmandu just before noon on 25 April 2015. The quake was the lead story on all of the news channels. It's hard to describe how I felt—sort of numb, and really confused. I couldn't understand what I was seeing when my entire family had just left Kathmandu 20 hours earlier.

I knew from the early reports that thousands of people would have been killed and that many more would die. I knew that those dead would include some of my friends. My mind raced through all the people I knew in Nepal, and every single one of those thoughts scared me. Rob and Marie-Kristelle were somewhere on Everest. Were they OK? God, were they even alive?

As more footage started to come through on the news, the damage was even worse than I'd feared. There were hundreds of buildings down in Kathmandu. It was a scene of total devastation. Then up flashed the remains of the Monkey Temple and there I saw what was left of the little rooftop cafe where I'd sat with Dylan on one side of me and Maya on the other, drinking Coke, chatting and laughing. How could that have only been two days ago? How could that pile of rubble be where we had sat?

My phone beeped again. This time it was my pilot fleet manager Gus Black asking where I was . . . Then another beep, Air New Zealand's chief pilot and my old mentor,

Captain David Morgan. 'I understand you are in Nepal. Please advise if you are OK or need help.'

I let them both know that we were out of Kathmandu and we were all OK.

Until that point, I hadn't even thought of posting on social media to let people know we were OK, so I did that straight away. The responses from our friends and family showed just how worried they'd all been about us.

Then came reports of a huge avalanche ripping through the south base camp. I knew I needed to get out of the hotel room and away from the TV.

Twitter was alive with direct reports from people in Nepal. I saw one tweet that said, 'Just felt a huge earthquake here at Everest base camp on the north side. I hope my friends on the south are OK.'

I knew this was really bad. There are actually two base camps on Mount Everest—the north-side one is in Tibet and the south-side one is in Nepal. The northern one is in the middle of a valley and is quite far from the neighbouring mountains, but the one on the south side sits in a sort of amphitheatre surrounded by giant mountains. When I was climbing Everest, I sat at the south base camp and listened to the rumbling roar of avalanches as they peeled off those mountains. They seemed really close and the only comfort was the fact that Everest base camp had never been hit by an avalanche in its 65-year history . . . but this was different.

Then came reports of a huge avalanche ripping through the south base camp. I knew I needed to get out of the hotel and away from the TV. I was devastated and the kids were upset.

They had been watching the news with us and had seen it all unfolding. We knew that Dr Rob was somewhere on Everest, and none of us knew if he was alive or dead.

Wendy and I took the kids out and we walked around the shops quite aimlessly, trying our best not to think about what was happening back in Nepal. I found it really hard not to look at my phone for updates, especially about Everest.

I got a message from my friend Mike Davey in the UK. He'd heard from Dr Rob's parents, who said that Rob and Marie-Kristelle were at Camp 1 on Everest when the earthquake struck. Other than that, they knew nothing.

Gradually, more information came out about the avalanche. There were 21 people killed, including ten Sherpa. The names of the dead began appearing on my Facebook feed. My heart sank when I read the name of a Sherpa I knew. His name was Pasang Temba.

Pasang had been the cook on my Everest expedition and he was an amazing man. He was deaf and couldn't speak, and he worked as a cook at base camp and up at Camp 2. He made this amazing pizza one night with different cheeses and yak meat on it. He was so proud of it when he brought it into the dining tent.

When I heard about Pasang's death I was determined to help his family.

After summiting, I sat with him at Camp 2 and we talked using makeshift sign language and hand gestures. I told him that I'd made the summit, and he smiled, made a loud noise and patted me on the back.

I learned later that he was in the cook tent when the

earthquake struck. While the other Sherpa heard the avalanche coming and lay down, Pasang couldn't hear it. He was standing up when the shockwave hit, and was killed by chunks of snow and ice. He left behind a wife, two daughters and a grandson. He was the income earner for the family. Cruelly, the earthquake had destroyed his family's home as well. When I heard about Pasang's death I was determined to help his family.

Finally, I got the good news I'd been so desperately waiting to hear: Mike Davey let me know that Rob and Marie-Kristelle had climbed from Camp 1 to Camp 2 and they were safe. We were all so relieved.

Camp 2 was much less likely to be struck by an avalanche triggered by one of the hundreds of aftershocks that were now hitting the country. While our friends were safe at Camp 2, there was no way that they could safely climb back down and off the mountain as the ladders across Khumbu icefall had been badly damaged and three Sherpa had already been killed trying to fix them.

It took three days before it was safe enough for a fleet of helicopters to begin evacuating climbers from Camp 2. The 30 climbers stranded there were flown to safety by some incredibly brave pilots. The climbers were only allowed the clothes on their backs, their money and their passports due to the weight restrictions onboard—that is how close they were to the maximum performance limits of the choppers.

I was so relieved when I knew that Rob and Marie-Kristelle were safe, so it was with a slightly lighter heart that Wendy, the kids and I flew home to New Zealand. We never could have imagined that our trip to Kathmandu would have such a devastating ending.

CHAPTER 15

RECOVERY

Once we got home, I had quite a few people contact me to ask how they could help the people of Nepal. I needed some time to think about it, but I wanted to do something. The kids seemed to handle coming home well. I don't think the reality of the earthquake really sunk in for Dylan and Ethan. Maya, however, was a different story; she seemed more upset.

A week after the first earthquake, I heard that another huge earthquake had hit and its epicentre was in Namche. There were reports that the whole village had been wiped out. I was terrified—Namche was like a second home to me. Surely it couldn't be gone. When the kids heard about this earthquake, they were all really worried about Palden and his family.

The first thing I did was get in touch with Palden to see if he was OK. He quickly let me know that the damage from the quake was very bad, and his lovely four-storey tea house was now on a bit of lean, but he assured me that no buildings in the town had collapsed.

At first, I was just really relieved to hear this news. Then I got a bit angry at the media for having reported something that turned out not to be true. I get that, for some people, these reports are just a thing that happened in another country, but for me they were really upsetting as I knew so many people who were directly affected.

At first, I was just really relieved to hear this news. Then I got a bit angry at the media for having reported something that turned out not to be true.

Of all of our children, Maya was the most troubled by the news of the earthquake in Namche. One evening, she kept coming out of her room and asking me questions. 'How much are plane tickets to Nepal, Dad?' Then, 'How much does a porter cost to trek from Lukla to Namche? How much does it cost to hire a Sherpa guide?'

After several such questions, I asked what she was doing and she said she would tell me later.

A few hours passed before she came out of her room again. She was holding a huge spreadsheet on which she had worked out all the costs of her and me flying to Kathmandu and taking our huge family tent as baggage, then getting some Sherpa and porters to carry it up to Namche, where we would set it up.

Her plan was to ask some of my friends who were medical professionals to volunteer and set up a triage centre, where they could treat some of the wounded and injured Sherpa. She was extremely serious about all this.

I was so proud of her for caring so much about our friends in Nepal. It broke my heart to have to tell her that, even though it was an amazing idea, we couldn't do it. I tried to explain to her that a team of surgeons from the UK had already flown to Nepal and offered their services, only to find that there wasn't anywhere for them to work because the damage was so great. Maya was pretty shocked to hear this, and was sad when I explained that, even though they were trying to help, they were actually taking up precious resources like food and water just by being there in Nepal. After a week, they realised they couldn't do anything and went home again.

While Maya was trying to work out what to do to help, I was looking for a way to make use of all the offers of help I'd received so we could do something for Pasang Sherpa's family.

My friend Haley offered to help me fundraise and suggested we have a movie night. I thought it was a great idea and I was even happier when she offered to help organise it. I booked two movie theatres—one showing *Pitch Perfect* and one showing *The Gunman*—each with 600 seats, and charged people $25 a ticket. No one minded paying double the normal price as they knew the profit was going to a good cause. The tickets sold out really quickly.

The movie night went very well and donations flooded in. One person donated $5000, which was unbelievably generous. Our final total raised was NZ$16,000. I opened a separate bank account for all the donations that were coming in, and then started to worry that the Inland

Revenue Department might see it as extra income. I called them to find out what I needed to do and, to my surprise, they were super helpful. They gave me lots of advice and made it clear that tax wasn't going to be a problem at all. They just wanted to see that the money would leave the account and go to people in Nepal.

The truth was I didn't know exactly what I was going to do with the money, but I was determined to help and I wanted to build Pasang Temba's wife and family a new house. I called a number of Sherpa friends in Nepal, and they reckoned it would cost about NZ$12,000 to rebuild the house. We could use the rest to help other Sherpa families.

I called Kami Sherpa, the non-elected leader of Pangboche. Kami is the man who climbing groups talk to when they want to organise Sherpa teams for Everest expeditions. I asked him if I could send the money directly to him. He said I could, and promised to ensure that it was all used to rebuild the house. He thanked me for helping, then told me that Pasang Temba's wife was his sister. I knew he would do his best to help her out, and I was happy that the money raised would be going directly into rebuilding the house.

A few days later, my phone rang and I answered to hear a Scottish voice say, 'Is this Mike Allsop?'

I confirmed it was and asked who I was speaking to. The man introduced himself, then asked if I had given Pasang Temba's widow the money to rebuild her house.

When I said I had, he replied, 'So did I!'

We both went silent for a minute, then he asked me how I felt about it.

I feel very strongly that if someone is given cash as a donation for a specific cause, it's their duty to ensure that the money goes to that cause, which made this phone call a bit awkward. I thought for a few seconds, then asked if he knew what she was going to do with the extra money.

'She is going to build a second house—one she can rent out for an income. Are you OK with that?'

OK with it? I thought it was a brilliant idea. Now, not only would she have somewhere to live, but she'd also have a chance to earn some money to keep the family fed and warm—money that they wouldn't have had otherwise without Pasang. It felt like the perfect solution.

When the shaking started, he was standing in the kitchen of a tea house and he ran outside just as the building started to slide down the mountain.

With Pasang's family house underway, my thoughts turned to Nawang and his family in Kathmandu. At the time of the earthquake, Nawang had been guiding a group on a trek. When the shaking started, he was standing in the kitchen of a tea house and he ran outside just as the building started to slide down the mountain. One of his clients was having a shower and dived through a window of the disappearing house naked. He survived.

After the ground stopped shaking, Nawang and his six clients were left standing there with nothing but the clothes on their backs. Well, five of them did—one of them had nothing at all, not even his clothes.

Nawang told me he had climbed down the mountainside for hours, searching through the rubble for his clients' gear, so they would have some protection against the cold in the oncoming night. He also had to find his pack, as it had all the money in it for the expedition.

Eventually, he located his pack and a lot of the clients' gear as well, but he was exhausted and the rest of the team, while grateful to him, were all very frightened. As night fell, they settled into makeshift shelters made from tarpaulins that Nawang had found. No one slept well on account of the huge aftershocks that kept hitting, each of them triggering landslides in the mountains around them. The noise was horrendous and Nawang said he really thought he was going to die.

The next morning, it became clear that there wouldn't be any evacuation helicopters available for quite some time. Their only choice was to walk back to the nearest road. It took them ten days. Each day they walked for as long as they could and each night they slept rough, begging for food from anyone who was willing or able to help. It turned out that having money made no difference as there was barely any food anywhere. Everyone was just doing their best to survive.

Each day they walked for as long as they could and each night they slept rough, begging for food from anyone who was willing or able to help.

Having made his way home, Nawang was faced with another tough situation. With Everest closed for the rest of the season and the country's infrastructure severely damaged, no one was coming to visit, which meant there was no work for him as a trekking guide. We'd been emailing each other and I knew how stressed he was about having no means to support his family.

I had an idea and wrote to him with a job offer. I asked him to go to Pangboche for a couple of weeks to oversee the building process of Pasang's family house. He could be my eyes there and send me photos, so that I could show the people who had donated exactly where their money went.

At the same time, I asked him to take some of the money I'd raised to two other families who were struggling to survive. This job meant Nawang had enough money for his family to survive through the rest of the trekking season, even if he didn't have any other work.

A few months later, I got the chance to check in with Nawang in person and to see the damage in Kathmandu for myself. For a while, I'd been talking to a production company called August about an idea I'd had for a television show named *Everest Rescue*. It would involve filming the work that helicopter pilots like Jason do to get people off the mountains.

One of the producers, Cass Avery, called and asked me to go to Nepal with her to discuss the logistics of filming, negotiate contracts and arrange some introductions. She reckoned it would be a good idea to have an airline pilot and an Everest summiteer on her side while doing these negotiations.

I checked my roster and I had nine days off in a row right when she wanted me to be there. It was a coincidence, but a good one. Then I realised that Maya's eleventh birthday was right in the middle of the time I'd be away. There was absolutely no way I was going to miss that, so I explained to Cass that I couldn't go and told her why.

Her response surprised me. 'Why don't you bring Maya with you?'

I said I'd talk to Wendy about it and let her know.

Wendy was happy for me to take Maya. She knew how important it was for Maya, especially given how upset our girl had been about the earthquake.

Having made the decision, I had a look at flights for us. I thought that because Maya still qualified for a child's fare, it would be a bit cheaper. Ahhh, no. Her flight ended up costing me pretty much all of what I earned by going up to Nepal to do the negotiations . . . but it was totally worth it.

I was a bit nervous visiting Kathmandu only three and a half months after the earthquake, so I made a few enquiries. I was told that the aftershocks had died down, and the hotels I called assured me that they had been inspected by engineers and many of them had safety compliance certificates issued. Even so, I decided that this time we'd stay at the Radisson instead of our favourite Hotel Manaslu; I thought it would be safer to stay at a big hotel from an American chain, in case there were any aftershocks or new earthquakes.

▲

We set off for Nepal via Singapore and Delhi. Maya was very excited about returning to Nepal. After 28 hours of flying, we were delighted to see Rajan waiting for us. It's so nice to have someone meet you at the airport, no matter where you're landing.

As Rajan drove us into the city, we could see countless buildings that had been reduced to rubble. He told us that the ones that were roped off still had people buried under the rubble. I looked at Maya when he said this and I could tell she was sad, but she didn't ask any questions.

One of the huge walls that surrounded Narayanhity

Palace, which was the home of the last king of Nepal, had fallen over in the quakes. The army had been mobilised to rebuild it. One thing that really struck me as we drove through Kathmandu was that there was no one sitting around; everyone seemed to be working with a purpose, and that purpose was to rebuild the city.

One thing that really struck me as we drove through Kathmandu was that there was no one sitting around; everyone seemed to be working with a purpose, and that purpose was to rebuild the city.

Nawang, his wife, Dolma, and their daughter, Kusang, were waiting for us at the hotel. They took the girls off to play together while Cass and I went to a couple of meetings. Maya was so happy to see her friend again.

That evening, we had a business dinner and Maya came along. The Nepalese are so friendly towards children and they welcomed Maya warmly. The restaurant we were at had live music, and the businesspeople we were with gave Maya money to donate to the band. She had a ball.

The next morning, Nawang came to collect Maya again. While I was at meetings, Nawang was taking Maya to school with Kusang. The two girls happily went off to class together. In a school with 3000 students, Maya was barely even noticed.

Maya couldn't wait to tell me all about it that night. 'Dad, I went to school with all these Nepalese kids and we had lunch—1500 kids at a time in this big hall! And, Dad, we had steel trays and no cutlery. Guess what? We had to eat with only our right hand.' She could barely keep up with the words as they tumbled out of her mouth.

'And, Dad, you'll never guess what happened when the first 1500 kids had finished their lunch—they *hosed* down the dining hall! Then the next 1500 kids came in . . . It was *so* amazing, Dad!'

As Maya and I lay in our beds that night, she got a bit upset. The next day was her birthday and we'd be leaving Nepal. She wanted to stay there longer. I explained that we couldn't, and there were a few tears, but she understood.

In the morning, we woke up and called home to speak to Wendy, Ethan and Dylan. I had a few little birthday presents for Maya as well. Nawang, Dolma and Kusang came to say goodbye. It was sad to be leaving them in Kathmandu, especially knowing that Nawang had no work and no idea when his next trekking jobs would come.

Even though we were only in Nepal for three nights, I was so happy that I'd been able to bring Maya on this trip with me. She seemed a bit less worried about her friends and about Kathmandu.

CHAPTER 16

A NEW FAMILY TRADITION

Now that all of the Allsop kids had hit the age of seven and done their trek to see Everest with their dad, and we'd done the trip as a family, it was time to think of a new family tradition to give the kids something to work towards, something to be excited about. The age-based thing had worked really well, and I admit I was quite surprised that the excitement of it had lasted right through until Dylan had his turn. I thought perhaps the novelty might have worn off for the kids by then, but I guess seeing his older brother and sister have their turn and knowing his would come soon enough kept Dylan's interest up.

At one of our dinners at Taiko, Wendy and I talked

about the possibility of taking each of the kids on another adventure when they turned 14. This time, the plan had a twist: it would be up to each of the children where we went and what we did. Whatever it was, it had to be completely outside the limits of what they thought was possible for them to do, but it also had to be safe and it had to have Wendy's stamp of approval. Oh, and it had to do good for someone else.

I believe kids are like rivers: you can't stop them or dramatically change their course, but you can gently change their flow.

We could both see the importance of helping the kids to push their limits as they got older. I really believe that the only limits people have are the ones they place on themselves. Our children had all seen me push my limits, but I wanted them to know what it felt like too. I knew that if they set their limits sky-high—and it is about *their* limits, not mine—they'd be amazed by what they could achieve. I knew that would help them to believe in themselves and go on to achieve even greater things.

I believe kids are like rivers: you can't stop them or dramatically change their course, but you can gently change their flow. It was with this in mind that Wendy and I agreed each of the children had to choose their own adventure.

Once we'd had time to think about the concept a bit, we sat down and talked to the kids about it. We explained that it was time for us to come up with a new family tradition, and that as each of them turned 14 they'd be able to choose their adventure. We outlined the rules that we'd come up with, and we told them they needed to dream about what they wanted to do. We made sure they knew they had plenty of time to think about different options and that there was no hurry for them to decide, as it would still be two years before Ethan turned 14. They all loved the idea and soon the possibilities started to flow. Skiing in Canada, going to Disneyland, and sightseeing in London were the first things that they came up with. We had to gently explain that it must be an adventure that pushed their limits; something they didn't think they could do. The penny dropped and they started talking about Kilimanjaro and Machu Picchu.

With the kids' minds fizzing, I started planning another trek to Everest base camp. My Sherpa friends needed the work and Nepal needed the tourists, so I'd decided to guide a group in late 2016.

I knew that Iswari and his team at Himalayan Guides would have everything under control for me in Nepal, but I still had a ton of work to do organising everything at this end. I had travel arrangements to make, gear lists to send out and plenty of questions to answer. This time, I'd be taking a full group of 18 people, and unlike the last two groups they weren't all from Air New Zealand. Sure, there were some people from work, including the chief medical officer, Ben Johnston. There were also friends of friends, a few businesspeople, and the winner of a competition run by Flight Centre at one of their global events.

While I was working on all of this, Maya came in one day and said, 'Dad, I've been thinking about my 14-year-old adventure and I want to go to base camp. Can I jump the queue and go before Ethan? I'll be twelve and a half when you go there next time.'

I thought about it for a moment, mostly flicking through all the potential problems her request could create. 'Maya, you've been to Nepal three times and to high altitude twice. You know you'll make base camp. It's not an impossible thing for you to do. You need to think outside the box a bit more and come up with some unique ideas that seem impossible.'

I was gobsmacked. How on earth had an almost-12-year-old come up with that idea?

I knew it would be a huge order for her, but I felt strongly that she needed to come up with something bigger. Plus, it bought me a bit of time!

A few days later, Maya came in again and said, 'Dad, how about we take two stand-up paddleboards to base camp? Then we can find a lake or river that we can paddleboard on. It would be the world's highest SUP.'

I was gobsmacked. How on earth had an almost-12-year-old come up with that idea? 'That sounds great, Maya! Have you thought about how we will get a paddleboard up to base camp?' I asked.

'Of course, Dad. We'll take our inflatable ones and use Gurman's yaks.'

She really had thought this through. 'And what about the helping other people part?' I asked.

'Yeah, not sure on that one yet, Dad.'

It was then that I remembered eight widows who lived in Upper Pangboche. Lama Geshe had told me about them. They had all lost fathers, husbands and sons to the mountains. I suggested to Maya that she could raise money for these women and use it to replace the roofs on their houses, which were in extremely poor condition. In some cases, they just had slates on top of plastic shopping bags, which provided a crude moisture barrier.

So Maya told all of our family and friends about what she was planning and she managed to raise US$500. She thought it was a great idea . . . but there were still a couple of hurdles. The first of which was Ethan. He was 22 months older than his sister, so if I took her on this adventure he'd miss out on being the first of the kids to have his 14-year-old trip. Wendy and I talked about how best to approach it and decided I should sit down and talk to him about it.

I explained that Maya had come up with her idea, and that—if he agreed—she could come and do it while I was on my next trek to base camp. I was quite surprised to find that he was OK with it, mostly because he hadn't decided what he wanted to do when his turn came. He could see the sense in Maya going first. He never mentioned it, but I think deep down he knew that I would follow through and he would get his turn.

The next hurdle was seeing if Maya could get time off school. Some of the trip was in the school holidays, but I still had to talk to her teachers and make sure it was OK if she took some time off. In the end, we did a deal with her school dean. If Maya came with me, she would do a speech about the trip in front of the whole school when she got back.

The thought of it terrified Maya, but I just kept reassuring her that it was all part of the adventure and challenge. I told her that she'd be fine standing up in front of everyone, and the more I reassured her the more she believed it herself. Eventually, she agreed to do the speech and got the time off school.

Maya's mission was on.

CHAPTER 17

DREAMING BIG

Before I take a group to Nepal, we all get together for dinner so we can discuss logistics, talk about our goals and do a bit of team bonding. Prior to our team dinner for this trip, two of the team got 12 suitcases of clothes shipped up to Auckland from Christchurch. The plan was that we would split them between all of our bags and take them to Kathmandu where they would be donated to an orphanage for people who needed them.

I must have looked like I was moving house—the car was full of suitcases and there were even a couple tied to the roofrack! But all of the others agreed to take a case home and repack the contents ready to go to Nepal. Most of us were flying China Southern Airlines, which has a luggage allowance of two 23-kilogram bags per person, so it was a good opportunity to take the extra gear.

On our flight from Auckland to Guangzhou, I managed to embarrass Maya. As the meal service came around, I asked the flight attendant what the meal choices were. He looked at me, paused and then made these sounds: 'Baaa, baaa. Swish, swish.'

Then he cracked up laughing, and one of the other flight attendants turned around and said, 'I'm really sorry. He doesn't speak English. The choices are lamb or fish.'

I grinned back at the first flight attendant, and replied, 'Baaaa, please!'

He burst out laughing again, and handed me my meal.

It was only then that I heard Maya muttering under her breath, 'Oh, Dad, you are *so* embarrassing.'

Yep, she's nearly a teenager, I thought.

After a very smooth three-hour connection in Guangzhou, we landed in Kathmandu. All but two of the trekking team were on the same flight, so it took a bit of organising to get everyone through customs and on to the bus that Iswari had waiting for us.

I always say that arriving at Hotel Manaslu is like seeing an old friend, but this time I really did see an old friend. As we were checking in, who should walk in but Dr Rob! I had no idea he was going to be there. Maya and I were both super excited to see him, so there were hugs all round. He was in Kathmandu arranging a trek that he would be guiding.

While the rest of the team settled into their rooms, we did what seems to be Allsop tradition now—we headed for the pool. Before I knew it, Maya and Rob had pumped up one of the inflatable SUPs and were playing on it in the pool. This kept us all entertained for several hours.

At dinner that night we were joined by Mingma Sherpa, a very famous Sherpa who has climbed Everest six times and K2 twice, among many others. His current goal is to summit all 14 of the world's 8000-metre-plus peaks.

I could see something hanging underneath the helicopter as it flew. It slowly dawned on me that the thing was a person.

Not only is Mingma an amazing climber, but he's also incredibly brave. He showed me a video that a climber had taken on Dhaulagiri, which at 8167 metres high is the world's seventh highest mountain. In the video, I could see a tiny speck flying through the mountains. As it got bigger, I realised it was a helicopter. Then, as it came close, I could see something hanging underneath the helicopter as it flew. It slowly dawned on me that the thing was a person.

My mouth dropped and I looked at Mingma. He was grinning, 'It's me! And all with no training.'

What?!

I watched as the helicopter lowered Mingma onto the ridge next to the climber who was filming. Then the video ended.

Mingma was almost blasé as he explained what had happened. 'A helicopter turned up at Everest base camp and the crew were asking for the lightest Sherpa. Someone pushed me forward as I'm only forty-eight kilos. They then flew me to Dhaulagiri, put me on the longline beneath the chopper and I got to the climber. He had a broken leg.'

I looked at Mingma and stuttered, 'No training?'

He laughed. 'No training, Mike.'

Unbelievable.

After a great first night with the crew in Kathmandu, we were rudely awoken at 5.30am by Hotel Manaslu's resident rooster. To make things even worse, this guy has the weirdest, most stuffed-up crow. He starts off making these half-pitch, scratchy noises. I lay there almost feeling sorry for the bird, thinking, *Come on, fella. You can do it!*

Then, after a dozen attempts, he finally let out a full-on, proud rooster crow. 'Yes! That's it, boy.'

There were a few minutes of silence. I hoped that, happy with his morning's effort, the rooster would get on with his day. But this boy had other ideas. He went right back to square one with his half-pitch, scratchy noise then worked his way up to a good crow. This continued for the next hour and a half.

Finally, at 7am, I pulled my head out from under the pillow where I'd tried to escape the sound of the Manaslu rooster, and it was time to rise and shine.

When Maya got up, her first words were, 'Oh my god, Dad. That rooster!'

We spent the next 20 minutes imitating it as we got ready for the day.

Our first full day in Kathmandu followed a well-worn path—filling our tummies at Mike's Breakfast, then off to Shona's to stock up on any last-minute gear that might be needed. Shona was so happy to see Maya again and made a real fuss of her.

Then it was on to dinner at Kilroy's of Kathmandu, which is a local institution. It was a lovely night so we sat outside on the roof with only candles to light the tables, and surrounded by a potted garden and a huge tree as a canopy.

Sadly, Kilroy's has since closed down and that was the last time I got to eat there.

We all caught rickshaws back to the hotel after dinner. As usual it turned into a bit of race, with much banter as one overtook the other. At one point, Maya said, 'Dad, you pedal. Then we can go faster!'

I wasn't sure about that, but I asked the rickshaw driver if I could take over pedalling for a bit. He agreed, happy to have a rest!

I was a bit wary about driving the rickshaw, as I'd heard about a couple of climbers who had paid their driver to let them have a go, then crashed into a power pole. The rickshaw was wrecked and the driver was in tears—he'd just lost his only source of income. Thankfully, the two blokes did the right thing and went and bought the man a brand-new rickshaw. When they delivered it to his house, he cried again—but this time they were happy tears.

Fortunately, I didn't have to go rickshaw shopping the next morning, and the driver not only got a rest but also a decent tip from us for being such a good sport! And we did manage to go a little faster.

After getting back to the hotel, the rest of the team called it a night and Maya went to bed, while Rob and I sat out on the balcony, drank beer and chatted. It was so good to have this unexpected chance to catch up with him.

A late night did nothing to dampen the buzz I felt when I met with the rest of the group very early the next morning. In fact, it was so early, we all had packed breakfasts from the hotel as the restaurant wasn't open yet.

Nawang was there to help get everyone organised, and I was delighted to have him alongside me on the team. He'd managed to get through the quiet period after the earthquake and was happy to be back working with trekking groups.

It was before dawn, the city was still asleep and there was no one around. The dogs had all exhausted themselves barking all night and the stage was now open for the roosters to start crowing, including our mate. It felt like the sleeping giant of a city was slowly waking up.

After the calm pre-dawn quiet of the city, the mass of people and the buzz of activity at the airport was a bit of a shock. As usual, Rajan was with us, helping everyone get to where they needed to be with minimum fuss.

As soon as boarding commences, everyone rushes to get the seats on the left because that's where they'll get the best views of the Himalaya.

One thing that first-time visitors to the airport can find a bit weird is the process of being weighed along with their baggage. There's a very good reason for this. A few years ago, a flight that had just taken off from Kathmandu to Lukla is thought to have hit a bird, which then caused an engine fire. The pilots attempted to turn back to make an emergency landing, but didn't make it. The plane crashed, killing all 19 people on board—seven from Nepal, seven from the UK and five from China. As part of the investigation into the crash, it was found that the plane was overloaded, which could have contributed to the crash. Since then, Nepalese airlines insist on weighing everything so they can accurately report the on-board loads. In some ways, this helps allay my fears about the flight to Lukla, but I still worry a bit every time.

While the airlines do everything they can to make sure the plane is evenly weighted, I can't say the same for the passengers. As soon as boarding commences, everyone rushes to get the seats on the left because that's where they'll get the best views of the Himalaya, but eventually every seat gets filled up.

Our ride up to Lukla was smooth, as the weather was nice and clear. We got a great view of the mountains on the way up, and we got to Lukla without any drama.

As the pilot began the final approach, the flaps went out, the landing gear went down, and the propellers went to full fine pitch. We were committed to landing. As the aircraft crossed the end of the runway, the pilot flared the aircraft—pulling the nose up to minimise the stress on impact—then put extra power on and flared it again; a very skilful technique. We touched down firmly.

Maya and I were delighted to be back in Lukla, and couldn't wait for our compulsory hugs from Dawa over at Paradise Lodge. Our new adventure had begun.

▲

My third guided trip to Everest base camp was underway! I was looking forward to getting to know everyone on the team, and I couldn't wait to catch up with some of my friends along the way. Best of all, I had Maya there to experience it all with me.

We also had another new team member. I'd asked Nawang's wife, Dolma, if she wanted a job on this trek, just in case a team member got seriously sick and I had to leave Maya. Originally, I'd planned for Dolma to join us from Pangboche to base camp and back, but she was so excited that she decided to come along all the way from Lukla. I was a bit worried it would change the dynamic between me and Nawang, but I quickly discovered that Dolma had an amazing knowledge of the area's history and a lovely way of sharing it.

The first day's walk from Lukla to Monjo was about eight hours. We took it pretty easy as there was quite a lot for the people who hadn't been here before to absorb. The route goes along the side of a valley with a few ups and downs, but nothing too grunty.

The next morning, we climbed up to Namche Bazaar, with the requisite stop at the lookout so everyone could get their first view of Everest. I just love that moment when people realise they're seeing the world's highest mountain for the first time.

Of course, at Namche, we all stayed with Palden and Tsering at Namaste Lodge. The lodge is four storeys tall and the original building is very old. Over the years, a few new additions have been added. Some of the doors are very low and many a tired trekker has bumped their head on the doorways. As a result of the earthquake, Palden's lodge got a bit of an extra lean to it, but he had managed to re-level it and he'd also had the outside replastered by the time we arrived.

Palden and Tsering greeted us all warmly, and hot drinks and popcorn were handed out to all of our team. Later, Tsering took Maya into the kitchen and gave her a job: peeling potatoes for dinner. Maya loved being able to help out in the kitchen and stayed there for a few hours, chatting to Tsering as she worked.

I spent the afternoon arranging rooms and talking to the other trekkers. I always try to find out if anyone's not feeling well, and will check in to make sure they've had enough to eat and drink. I also try to convince them to rest, which isn't always easy when they want to go out and explore.

This stop in Namche is all about acclimatising, and to help with that we trekked nice and slowly over the hill to Khumjung the following day. At the top of the ridge, I stopped and pointed out Ama Dablam, the Lhotse ridge and Everest. It's a magic trio.

After a brief visit to Khumjung School, it was time for lunch. I'm always really careful when it comes to eating anywhere that I'm not super sure about, as I don't want to risk anyone getting sick. As a result, I recommend that everyone has Rara instant-noodle soup.

Back in Namche later that day, I took the team to the Sherpa Museum. On the way up, Maya asked if she could show everyone around and be their guide. I thought that was a great idea.

The museum has exhibits about Sherpa culture, including a replica Sherpa home, so visitors can learn a bit about life in the area. It also has a whole section about climbing Everest, and a great selection of photographs of Namche Bazaar. Outside there's a statue of Tenzing Norgay, who summited Everest with Edmund Hillary in 1953.

Maya stood in front of the statue and told the team about Tenzing Sherpa. She did a really good job and I was amazed at the confidence that it took for her to be able to do that. Afterwards, she stood and answered everyone's questions about the mountains and the region. Maya was a complete natural and had no trouble coming up with the right answers. I could barely believe that she was the same kid who was so nervous about having to speak in front of her school—I knew she'd ace it now.

▲

That evening at dinner, I told the team about Maya's plans for her adventure, especially the part about giving back to the community and how she had chosen to help the widows. The team were really moved hearing about these women and they all wanted to help as well.

To buy and transport one piece of roofing iron to Pangboche costs US$20. Soon I had team members wanting to donate two sheets of iron, then another person donated five sheets and one person was so moved they donated US$500 worth of iron. In the end, Maya raised another US$1500 to buy new roofing iron. This was absolutely huge for the people receiving it.

▲

After another night at Namaste Lodge, we set off for Pangboche. It's a long day's trekking so I always try to be on the track before 7.30am, but that usually turns into 8am and sometimes 8.30am.

We stopped at Kyangjuma to see Tashi. She was so happy to see Maya and me. She took Maya by the hand and led her to the jewellery she had laid out for sale. Tashi pointed to various pieces and asked Maya if she liked them. When Maya nodded that she liked one of them, Tashi gave it to her as a little gift. It was so sweet seeing the bond between them.

Then, of course, there was Maya the dog. The two Mayas formed a mutual appreciation society and happily fussed over each other.

Tashi served popcorn and tea to the whole crew, and

pretty much everyone fell a little bit under her spell!

For the next two hours, we hiked straight downhill to the valley floor. It always seems strange to be walking downhill after having spent so many hours climbing. At the bottom of the hill, on the banks of the Dudh Koshi river, is the village of Phungi Thenga.

I have an awesome technique for using horrible toilets when I'm in the wild. I wait until I am absolutely busting—like, really dying to go, but just before the point of sweating— and then any toilet seems like heaven.

We stopped at one of the village's two tea houses, where Nawang had arranged a lunch of vege fried rice and a vegetable noodle dish for everyone. This was great, as it was fresh and in bulk; the Sherpa served it out of big pots to everyone at the table.

As I finished my lunch, I realised that I needed to go to the bathroom, and it was number twos. Now, I have an awesome technique for using horrible toilets when I'm in the wild. I wait until I am absolutely busting—like, really dying to go, but just before the point of sweating—and then any toilet seems like heaven. The only real issue is timing—you can't risk leaving it too long. Unfortunately, on this occasion, my timing was slightly off. As I waddled, penguin-like, over to the square-boxed long-drop toilet, all I could think was, *I hope I don't have an accident . . .*

To my horror, when I got there, there was a queue. *Arghhh!* I started to sweat as I waited in line. When my turn finally came, I went into the toilet and realised that the cracks between the wood were so big that if anyone outside got too close, they'd be able to see exactly what was going on. I guess it was good for ventilation.

Being seen was the least of my worries by this point, though. As quickly as I could, I turned the piece of wood that was the door lock and undid my pants, then squatted over the hole, making sure I avoided contact with all the misfires around it, then . . . heaven. Best toilet in the whole world.

As I carefully stood up afterwards, I could see through the walls that one of the trekkers, a German, was walking towards the toilet. Then I heard the door being yanked— hard.

'Hello!' I shouted, but it was too late. He'd pulled the door so hard that he broke the wooden lock.

Pants and underpants around my ankles, I managed to quickly turn and preserve some small shred of my dignity, white arse fully facing Mr Germany.

He was so shocked that he froze, leaving the door wide open. I could hear a group of passing trekkers pissing themselves laughing at the sight of my white bum. In the end, I had to say, 'Hey, buddy, how about you shut the door?'

When I got back to the rest of the group, I told them the tale of my escapades and they howled with laughter. Toilet humour is something that bonds people on these treks, as most will end up with their own tale to share.

After lunch and a good laugh, we all tackled Tengboche hill. It's a beautiful climb, starting off with some switchbacks that lead into forest, which then gives way to beautiful rhododendron forest. Even in late autumn, the trees are lovely, but in spring, when they're in flower, they're truly magnificent.

Following a visit to the monastery, some prayers and lots of photos, we carried on towards Pangboche, which was a couple of hours' walk away. On the way, we passed through a village called Deboche. There's a small nunnery there, which is believed to be the oldest in Nepal. Whenever I see it, I'm reminded of a conversation I had with Lydia Bradey, who was the first woman to summit Everest without supplemental oxygen. She told me that monasteries get a lot of help in Nepal, but the nunneries usually miss out so the nuns live in very tough conditions.

Thankfully, the Deboche Project, an international charity that has heaps of climbers involved, has been set up to help the nuns there. The project's work has been life-changing.

As we left Deboche, Gurman came down the track with his horse. It was a nice surprise to see him. It turned out that Nawang had called and asked him to bring his horse down, as one of our party was struggling a little bit.

I introduced my old friend to the whole team, proudly telling them, 'This is Gurman Sherpa. He has climbed Everest four times, and Ama Dablam 16 times. We will be staying at his house in Pangboche.'

The team had spread out a bit, and each group had a Sherpa guide with them. I was relaxed and happy to be walking with Maya. As we passed the stupa we'd helped rebuild, I touched it, quietly glad to have been able to ensure that it was still there.

Maya and I strolled into Pangboche together. This was the first time I got to see the two new houses that had been built for Pasang Temba Sherpa's family. His widow was working outside as we walked past. I smiled and said hello, and she smiled back.

I told Maya that it was Pasang Temba's house, and she said, 'Dad, why didn't you tell her that you raised the money for her home?'

I explained to Maya that if Pasang Temba's widow knew what I had done then she would have felt compelled to thank me and there would have been a huge fuss. I didn't want that. 'The important thing is that we helped her, her daughter and her grandchildren, and gave them a little income and hope for the future. Can you imagine how sad it was for her, losing her husband?'

Maya looked sad as she thought about how hard things must have been for the woman. I could tell she really understood what I was saying.

By the time we got to Sonam Lodge, Maya and I were the last to arrive. I always try to make sure I'm the tail-ender on my treks, as it means I know where everyone is. It was great to find everyone happily settled in, drinking tea and ordering food.

The following morning, I went up to Lama Geshe's. I had heard that he still wasn't well, so I wanted to check whether it would be OK to take the team to see him for a blessing. I spoke to his daughter, Tashi, and she told me to bring the team up.

Lama Geshe put a small cord necklace around my neck, tied a knot and we slowly touched heads. Once again, I had the sense that I was in the presence of greatness.

Nawang organised white prayer scarves for everyone and I explained to the team that they were to roll a small donation up in the scarf and give it to Lama Geshe, all while keeping their heads low to show him respect.

We slowly walked up to his house and waited outside until we were told it was OK to go in and see him. Maya and I went first, and found Lama Geshe sitting there in his spot, smiling just as he always did.

Tashi motioned for us to come forward. I went first and bowed my head. Lama Geshe put a small cord necklace around my neck, tied a knot and we slowly touched heads. Once again, I had the sense that I was in the presence of greatness.

Maya moved forward next and there was a discussion between Lama Geshe and Tashi. 'My father remembers both of you,' Tashi explained.

I quietly took a photo of Maya looking straight at Lama Geshe as the light streamed in behind him, his hands open and facing upwards as he blessed her.

The rest of the team slowly came in, and each gave their scarf to Lama Geshe and received a necklace in return. Then we drank sweet Sherpa tea that Lama Geshe's wife brought out for us.

Then it was time for Lama Geshe to begin our formal blessing. He had a number of blessings and I had heard a few different ones over the years, but this time he gave us the same one he gave me before I climbed Everest. The hair on the back of my neck stood on end and tingles ran down my spine. I could clearly remember sitting in the same spot a decade ago, listening to the same blessing. Back then, in that moment, the build-up of stress and fear about climbing Everest had lifted off me. I'd been able to put all my physical, mental, emotional and spiritual energy into climbing the mountain. I cried that day too.

I lowered my head and the tears streamed down my cheeks. Two of my clients asked Lama Geshe to bless them, as they had just got married. He called them forward and did a special blessing for them, and they both cried as well. It wasn't just me who felt the significance.

Then the lama called Maya and me forward, and gave us a special blessing. The team slowly left the room with Maya and me the last to leave. I'm not sure why but, as I went to walk out, I turned around, returned to him, bowed my head and put out my hand. He took it with both of his and held it warmly. I looked at him and said, 'Thank you, Lama Geshe. Thank you.' I didn't know it then, but that would be the last time I would ever see him.

Afterwards, Maya returned to Sonam while Nawang and I went to visit Pasang Temba's wife. When we arrived, she was working in her vegetable garden. She knew Nawang and smiled at him. They spoke for a bit, then she smiled at me and went inside.

I took a few photos, then she came out with a silk scarf. I bowed my head and she placed it around my neck. She looked me in the eyes and said a simple thank you. I smiled, then Nawang and I headed back to the tea house.

It was perfect. I didn't want her to feel she had to make a big deal of me helping her—her thank you, her smile and seeing her working in the garden were enough. And I'm sure everyone who gave money to help her and her family would have felt the same way.

CHAPTER 18

BASE CAMP

After lunch, we left Pangboche for Pheriche, which is a lovely, quite gentle three-hour walk away. Dolma told us that she grew up in a village not far from there called Chukhung. As we walked along she told us a little bit more about her life. She'd lived in a one-room house with her parents and her older sister. Her father was a climbing Sherpa, so he was away a lot during spring and autumn, the climbing seasons. Her mother looked after the girls and the family yaks while he was gone.

Dolma was only a year old when her father was killed in an avalanche on Annapurna. He had a small life insurance policy, but as he wasn't officially married to her mother the money had instead gone to his brother, who kept it for himself.

With no income, Dolma's mother and the two girls had

to move out of their house and ended up living in a tiny yak hut with a thick curtain instead of a door. It is almost impossible to see how a young Sherpa mother could have survived herself in such harsh conditions, let alone keep two children warm as well. But she did.

One day a passing trekker noticed Dolma and her sister. She stopped to talk to them and was shocked to see how they were living. When she got home, the woman sent a package of warm clothes to Dolma's mother. In it was a pair of denim overalls. As a baby, Dolma wore these with the crotch cut out of them so she could go to the toilet easily. Then, once she was toilet-trained, the crotch was sewn back up. The overalls were slowly extended as she grew and Dolma wore them until she was six years old. The package's sender was Anita Roddick, the businesswoman who set up The Body Shop.

Some years later, Anita trekked back to Chukhung to visit the family again. She was surprised to see that they still had very little, as she had sent them many parcels of clothing and goods since meeting them. Only one had arrived, the rest probably stolen by desperate families in similar circumstances. Roddick continued to support Dolma's family until she passed away in 2007.

While Dolma took the job of looking after Maya very seriously and stuck to her side a lot, Maya was at her happiest when it was just me and her hanging at the back of the group on our own. Sometimes we talked and talked like teenagers, other times we said nothing for ages, then just smiled at each other. We bonded in such a cool way. I loved having so much time with her, with no phones, no computers and no TV to distract either of us. I liked that she wanted to hang out with her dad in the Himalaya.

It's important to me that I am a father to my kids and not their friend. It might sound strange, but there is a difference. I can be their friend when they are adults, but until then they need me as their father. With that role comes a responsibility to provide guidance and advice, and sometimes to set boundaries. Besides which, I reckon that you can still be a fun, strong dad without trying to be your kid's friend.

▲

For the next two nights, we stayed at the Himalayan Hotel in Pheriche. Calling it a hotel might be a bit of a stretch, but still it was a nice lodge with an amazing three-sided dining room that always had a great big fire burning in it. They also have the best chilli chicken in the whole of the Khumbu Valley.

At Pheriche, the altitude is about 4200 metres, so it's starting to get very high. One of the reasons I like staying in Pheriche is that the Himalayan rescue doctors have a clinic there, so any if any of the team are having problems they can see an experienced doctor.

One member of our team, Karen, was struggling a bit. She said she was feeling sick, so I got her to go to the doctors. They suggested that she descend to lower altitude for her own safety. I knew she would be disappointed, so I had to have a difficult conversation with her about going back down to Gurman's place in Pangboche with one of the Sherpa, where she could wait for us to return in five nights' time. The alternative was to descend all the way back to Lukla and fly out.

Karen opted to go to Pangboche with Mingma. He was a young Sherpa who she'd spent a lot of time trekking with and they got on very well. I told her that it would be fine and I would sort it. I thought it would be perfect, as Mingma lived in Pangboche and he could introduce Karen to his mum and dad there.

I went to talk to Nawang about it, and he said straight away, 'No, Mike. Mingma will not want to do that.' He was sure that Mingma would want to finish the trek and go to base camp with the team.

I was a bit surprised, but asked him to speak to Mingma about it anyway, which he did.

'Sorry, Mike. Mingma says no. I will send another Sherpa, OK?'

'Nawang, it has to be Mingma as he gets on very well with Karen and it will be better for her. She is the client and they come first.'

Eventually, a slightly sulky Mingma agreed to take Karen back to Pangboche. All this was going to have a silver lining, but they just didn't know that yet.

Karen ended up getting on so well with Mingma and his family that they stayed in contact after she got back home. A couple of months later, Karen organised for Mingma to visit New Zealand. It wasn't easy—there were letters to the New Zealand government asking for assistance with Mingma's visitor's visa, which went to the Indian consulate and then to Nepal's head of immigration.

Finally, Mingma made it to New Zealand and Karen got to return the kindness he had shown her in an amazing way. She organised for him to stay with different team members off the trek all around the country, which was a pretty cool experience for him.

▲

The next day was an acclimatisation day, so we all went for a huge trek straight up to about 5000 metres. Once we got up there, we sat and had some snacks and enjoyed the view of the backside of Ama Dablam.

Back at our accommodation, it was time to just rest and chill out. The lodge had WiFi, so there was a flurry of social media activity as everyone updated their statuses and let their friends and family know they were OK.

I noticed that Maya didn't update her Instagram. She'd told me earlier that she was worried what the kids at her school would think of her being in Nepal trekking.

I noticed that Maya didn't update her Instagram. She'd told me earlier that she was worried what the kids at her school would think of her being in Nepal trekking. I knew she was a bit worried about getting mean comments, as she'd mentioned it to me a couple of times. I just reassured her that it doesn't matter what other people think of her; what matters is what she thinks of herself.

Trekking in October or November can be a little bit busy, so I always make sure that our accommodation is booked ahead of time—except for in Lobuche, which was where we were hoping to stay the following night. There isn't much phone coverage up there and it's really hard to get hold of anyone at the lodges. Nawang asked for a volunteer to run ahead, book our accommodation and then come back. It was an eight-hour return trip for a Sherpa, but there were several volunteers who had their eyes on the extra pay it would earn them.

The next day we all set off to Lobuche. Along the way, we

stopped for some Rara soup at a tea house in Dughla owned by a Sherpa called Mr T. At the top of Dughla hill, there's a memorial for all of the people who have lost their lives on Everest. There's a row of stone cairns that stretches out a long way. Each commemorates the life of someone who has died on the mountain. It's a very sobering place.

Maya asked a lot of questions about the cairns, who the people were, whether I knew them and then, the saddest question, 'Why are there so many?' She looked thoughtful as she realised that every cairn represented a person who had a mother, a father, and maybe a wife or a husband or children. They were all lost people.

We went for a little walk around, and Maya held my hand as we read some of the inscriptions.

Husband to Mary, father to Josh, Anna, Jess and Peter. Lost on Everest with his Sherpa at 8400m

Maya and I stood there very quietly, then Maya said, 'Dad, why don't we build a cairn for Pasang Temba?'

I told her it was a great idea and we gathered some rocks and built a small cairn. It felt really special. One day, I will go back and build it properly, complete with a plaque.

We were all a bit more sombre as we left the memorial on our way to Lobuche. At the highest point on the day's trek, we were up at about 5100 metres. This is where the rubber hits the road and things start to get a bit tougher.

At this kind of altitude, it's vital that everyone drinks enough water. I've seen a lot of people get sick because they haven't drunk enough. At this altitude, adults lose about 250 millilitres of water through normal breathing. This amount increases with the heavy breathing that is a result of the exertion of trekking at high altitude. Drinking enough water takes discipline. My secret is to always drink one litre during the night.

Our night at Lobuche was pretty unremarkable. Apart from a few tea houses and lodges, there really isn't much there. It is what it is—a place to spend the night on the way to base camp, where we were headed the next day.

The next morning everyone was excited. The mountains towered over us on every side. In the distance, we could hear the roar of avalanches. Every time we heard one, everyone would stop and try to spot it, but they are so far away it's rare that you ever actually see one.

Gorak Shep is the last village before Everest base camp. It's where Edmund Hillary's team set up the base camp for their climb in 1953. In those days, the Khumbu Glacier was much larger and came all the way down to Gorak Shep.

On my two previous expeditions to base camp, we've been able to stay with Iswari's teams up at the camp. This time, though, Iswari didn't have anyone climbing Everest, so we weren't able to do that. Instead, we would be spending a couple of nights at Gorak Shep.

A lot of trekkers get sick here, as it's so high and the air is so thin that their immunity finally gives up with the amount of bugs around. We stayed at Ang Tsering's lodge, and he was there to greet us when we arrived.

There had been a few helicopters around that morning, so I asked him about them. He said a young British girl had got sick and needed to be airlifted out. 'But she was OK because, as they put her in the helicopter, they were giving her a heart massage!' He made the CPR motion with his hands. That scared me a little bit and I was glad Maya didn't hear him.

The reality is that it's normal for pretty much everyone to show small signs of altitude sickness, like having a mild headache. Taking Diamox can decrease the symptoms, but only if your travel doctor has approved it. However, if you start vomiting, then it's time to head back down. Under no circumstance should you go any higher, and most importantly of all, take someone with you who can call a helicopter if necessary. I always carry a bottle of emergency oxygen for the team, just in case.

The team had a quick lunch at Gorak Shep, then we set off on the two-hour walk to base camp. A two-hour walk sounds easy, but it's not. Everyone was pretty exhausted when we got there. Someone had painted a sign on a rock that said 'Everest base camp', which was a great idea. It gives all the trekking groups a spot to focus on.

Arriving at base camp was a significant achievement for the team. This was their summit and the tears flowed a little.

Maya jumped on my shoulders and we snapped a photo. I was very proud of her. Base camp is at 5780 metres, and getting up there is not easy for anyone, let alone a 12-year-old. It showed me just how much guts and determination she has.

We all gathered around the Everest Base Camp rock and posed next to it and took photos.

Back in Gorak Shep, my thoughts turned to finding a lake that I had only seen on Google Earth. I really hoped it wasn't frozen, but I wasn't sure of our chances, as everything up here freezes.

At dinner, I was happy to see that everyone was hungry and eating plenty. Seeing how much people are eating is a really good way of measuring how they are feeling at altitude, because your appetite is the first thing that goes with altitude sickness. I was glad to see them refuelling, as the following morning we would be climbing Kala Patthar. It's a small trekking peak that rises above base camp by only a few hundred metres, but because of the altitude it's very tough. The climb would take two to three hours.

That night Maya said she was feeling tired and asked if it was OK if she stayed in bed while I climbed Kala Patthar with the team. I told her I thought that was a good idea.

While Maya stayed in her warm bed, the rest of us were awake at 3.30am and away from the lodge at 4am. With the team gathered, I warned them how cold it was going to be—a bone-chilling –20°C. Then I gave them a bit of a pep talk: 'Find your courage and strength. We stay together, one step at a time, and never, never give up.'

I got everyone in a circle and we held hands while one of the Sherpa lit some juniper bush and said a prayer. It sent shivers down my spine as it was the same prayer I had heard the Sherpa make when I was climbing Everest.

We set off slowly together into the night. The first few hours were OK and the team was doing well—just the usual problems like cold feet and hands. Nothing major.

As the day began to break, the team started to spread out. I found myself at the back and struggling a little. I was with one other trekker, and I was happy because it looked like I was staying back helping her!

She soon left me and I slowed right down. I started to get worried as I really felt like I was struggling. I couldn't work it out. Perhaps the stress of running a team and looking after Maya had got to me? Altitude is funny in that way— the smallest things can affect you. Or perhaps I had put on too much weight? I was about eight kilograms heavier than when I'd been running all the time, but I didn't think that would make much difference. Or perhaps I was getting too old to be doing this? My mind started to run away on me as I got slower and slower.

Then something clicked and I told myself to have some compassion. 'You are doing just fine. You are safe—just slow. Just relax and enjoy the mountains.'

With that I sat down, took a huge breath and looked at the magnificent view. Almost instantly I felt better and after a few minutes I began climbing again. It didn't matter what speed I was going; it was *my* speed. All the stuff I always tell my clients, I was now telling myself.

As I got to the summit, most of the crew were on their way back down. I knew the Sherpa team were looking after them, so I could just relax and enjoy my surroundings. Then the sun popped up over Nuptse, the mountain that neighbours Everest. It was just beautiful. The sunrise colours lasted only a few seconds, then the warm rays hit me. I inhaled and felt at peace as I reflected on it all. I just felt so very lucky in my life.

After a little while, I started the descent. Being on my own was really nice, as it gave me time to think. When I'm leading a trek, there are always questions to answer and plans to be made, so I try to build in some down time for myself. I also always have my own room to sleep in, while the others share rooms. As well as giving me my own space, it means that if someone is not well they can sleep in my room with me so I can reassure and look after them.

When I arrived back at the tea house, the team were all eating breakfast. Everyone was in the groove and comfortable. Maya was there too, playing cards and happy as.

CHAPTER 19

ON THE LAKE

Maya and I started getting all the paddleboarding gear ready. Boards, paddles, wetsuits, tent, towels, pumps . . . There was so much to think about.

The lake that we were planning to use was about a two-hour walk from Gorak Shep. It's next to the base camp for a mountain called Pumori. I was a bit concerned, as it had looked frozen from the top of Kala Patthar that morning. Maya and I chatted about the possibility that it could be frozen, and I reassured her not to be afraid to fail. In the end, we decided to head up to the lake and give it a go. After all, not trying is the only real failure. Given we were, as far as I knew, the first people to ever attempt this, it was pretty cool for Maya to even give it a try.

I'd talked through the possible risks with Dr Ben. He told me he'd just done a course in Norway about how to deal with ice emergencies. Talk about good timing!

Ben went through the best ways to reheat people who have fallen into icy water, just in case. The methods are: in a warm bath (not an option for us!); with warm tea, dry clothes and movement, like doing star jumps or squats (check!); hopping into a sleeping bag with another person for body-to-body heat (note to self: take a sleeping bag); or just movement alone.

I know there are probably people out there who reckon letting a 12-year-old girl go paddleboarding on a freezing lake in the Himalaya is a stupid thing to do, and I was well aware of the criticism I would get if anything went wrong. There are a lot of naysayers in the world who like to make their opinions known—and loudly. This is just a part of life. There will always be critics, but if we all focused on what the naysayers might think then no one would ever do anything.

The important thing for me was that Wendy fully supported what we were trying to do. We also had a full safety plan in place, a doctor with expertise in precisely this kind of environment with us, and an amazing team of locals right there too.

If anything went wrong, we were more than equipped to deal with it. Nawang had organised a tent for Maya to get changed in, a sleeping bag in case she got wet, and a big thermos of hot tea to help warm her up after she'd been out on the lake. I was also taking a second paddleboard and some ropes in case she needed to be rescued. We had a satellite phone so we could call a helicopter if things got really serious. I don't think you can be any better prepared than that.

Quite a crew of us gathered to head up to the lake. As well as me, Maya, Dr Ben, Nawang and the Sherpa, a few members of the team decided they'd come too. We all set off across the flat salt lake and up a little track. Not far from Gorak Shep, we found a memorial for Kiwi climber Rob Hall, who was killed on Everest in 1996 trying to save one of his clients. I had read so much about him and his climbs; he was such a legend and someone I looked up to. He had really inspired me during my climbing days, so I quietly said a little thank you to him as we stood there. As we trekked up towards Lake Pumori, I told Maya all about Rob Hall and how he'd given up his own life to save someone else's, and how after he died he'd been awarded the New Zealand Bravery Star.

As the climb got steeper, Maya started to struggle a bit. She had a bit of a moan about how hard it was. Before I'd even really thought about it, I said, 'Maya, this is getting too hard for you. Perhaps we should go back.'

Maya was shocked and I got a real telling-off. 'No, Dad! We are *not* giving up. No!'

And then she said it: 'Allsops *never* give up.'

Hearing her say that brought a tear to my eye. I was so proud, especially because those words had come out so naturally in the heat of adversity. I looked at her and said, 'You're right. Let's do this!'

By this time, there wasn't a track to follow, so we were making our own way over a moraine, which is a whole lot of loose rocks and boulders left behind by a glacier. I'm always nervous on moraines because one of my early mentors, Paul Scaife, told me that they are very dangerous and a lot of people get killed on them from shifting and falling rocks. I looked around and it seemed so harmless.

Nawang, Maya and I were trekking together as the rest of the team had gone on ahead and were over the next ridge and out of sight. As the boulders we were climbing over got bigger, I told Maya to either stick next to me or Nawang.

I also told Nawang that I didn't like moraines, so he agreed to stay close to Maya as well.

We got to a spot where we had to climb up and over some rocks that were about six metres high. If we were rockhopping at the beach at home, I wouldn't think twice about doing this sort of thing, but this was different.

I told Nawang that I'd go first and that he and Maya should stay at the bottom until I was safely at the top. As I started to climb, it all felt solid and there was no movement at all in the rocks. As I passed a huge rock the size of a car, I put my hand on it to push myself up. The next rock I grabbed felt solid but, as I pushed, it gave away and slid down into the huge rock I'd just passed. The big rock started to move as well. There was a deafening, low-pitched roar as it started to slide—and I knew Maya and Nawang were right below it. *Shit!*

I looked back and Maya was standing there, stunned. Nawang grabbed her and pulled her out of the way as this boulder of solid granite hit exactly where they had been standing. My heart pretty much stopped.

I shouted to them, and Nawang's calm voice came back. 'We're fine, Mike. We're fine.'

Thank god.

I climbed down and hugged Maya. 'Yeah, ah, let's not tell Mum about that one, eh?'

All three of us cracked up laughing, releasing some nervous energy.

When we set off again, I took ages checking every rock I touched while Nawang stuck like glue to Maya.

As we trekked up a ridge that we hoped would be the last, one of the others came up the other side and shouted down to us. 'It's frozen! It's frozen!'

My heart sank. I looked at Maya and said, 'It's not over until it's over. We'll just have to see for ourselves, OK?'

She looked at me and didn't say anything, but I could tell she was disappointed.

Then we crested the ridge and saw Lake Pumori laid out before us. It was beautiful. I could scarcely believe my eyes. I pointed and said to Maya, 'Look! It's *not* frozen!'

Maya screamed, 'YES!' Then she laughed and said, 'You should have gone to Specsavers!' All our disappointment had been the result of a misunderstanding. The guy had actually been shouting 'It isn't frozen!' but because of the wind we hadn't heard him properly.

Maya was absolutely fizzing—so much so that I had to get her to sit down for a bit to calm down. We talked through the excitement of seeing that the lake wasn't frozen, then discussed our plan.

There was a hive of activity by the lake. The Sherpa were putting up the tent, some of the others were inflating the boards and getting Maya's wetsuit ready, and Dr Ben was looking around the lake to work out the best spots for Maya to get in and out.

While Maya was really excited, a little voice in my head had started to make itself known: doubt. 'This is very serious. Are you sure you should let her do this?' it said. 'What if she falls in? Remember how you felt when that rock fell. Do you want to go through that again?'

I find when my brain starts doing stuff like that it's good to reach out to someone I trust, so I went over to talk to Dr Ben. I asked him what he thought, and he seemed really positive. He assured me that we had covered every aspect and if Maya fell in she would be OK.

He suggested that Maya put her foot in the water, so her body and brain knew how cold it was. The idea was that it would prevent her body from going into instant shock if she fell in, as her brain would know what to expect. I OKed this, but suggested that she put her hand in because her foot might take too long to warm up. Ben agreed.

I had also planned to do a recce first to see if there was any submerged ice, which could throw Maya off balance if she collided with it.

I couldn't help but think of the time the legendary endurance swimmer Lewis Pugh swam across this very lake in 2010. He was super experienced when it came to swimming in extremely cold water and had done a world-record swim at the North Pole. He'd said that, as he swam out into the lake, he could feel the energy starting to drain from his arms and legs, and that he gradually got slower and slower until he couldn't move his arms or legs and simply began to sink. He just couldn't move. He reckoned he knew he was going to drown. He took what he was sure was his last breath, then sank to the bottom of the lake. It was at this point he realised it was only about a metre deep and he stood up!

Despite all my fears, I knew that I had to have momentary courage, to be brave for a few seconds and then just encourage Maya to go for it. (Ironically, it would have taken the same momentary courage to decide to pull the pin and say that I didn't think it was safe enough for Maya to go ahead with her attempt.)

'Let's do it!' I said to Ben, then I walked over to the tent to help Maya get ready. The idea was that she'd get into her wetsuit, then we'd tape up the arms, legs and neck, so that if she did fall in she wouldn't get wet.

I was worried about the amount of energy she was expending just putting the westuit on, and with how excited she was. In the back of my mind, I knew that after all this we still had to hike for two hours to get back to Gorak Shep.

I was worried about the amount of energy she was expending just putting the westuit on . . . I knew that after all this we still had to hike for two hours.

I looked over to where the Sherpa were pumping up the boards. They were having real trouble getting them inflated. It took me a moment to realise that this was because the pumps were designed for use at sea level. Here at over 5000 metres there was only half the air pressure there is at sea level.

I took over pumping one board up. As I pushed down on the pump, I couldn't feel any air being forced into the board. Only when I pumped as fast as I could did any air go into the board, but at that altitude I could only work that quickly for a few seconds before I was exhausted.

One of the Sherpa tapped me on the shoulder and said, 'Mike, let us do it.'

The three of them were lined up ready to give it their all. I was so grateful for their help.

There even seemed to be a little competitive streak coming out as they each gave it their all, then collapsed on the dirt for the next one to take over.

It usually takes about five minutes to inflate the boards, but it took 30 minutes. This meant we now had another issue—daylight. We still had the two-hour walk back down the mountain, and I started to worry about what would happen if Maya was too exhausted to walk back.

Nawang was concerned about time as well, so I decided not to inflate the rescue board—we just didn't have the time. Instead, I would take Maya's board and go out onto the lake on my knees to check for submerged ice. Once I was sure it was clear, Maya would then go out and stand up and paddle for the record. I told her to make sure she stayed close to the shore, so that if she fell in she could get back to us easily or, if need be, I could jump in and grab her.

I took the board down to the water. I had my lifejacket on over my clothes and my paddle at the ready. Ben had picked a perfect spot for us to launch, and had cleared all the ice away from the edge of a big flat rock. I threw the board onto the water and it hit with a loud slap. This was it.

I took a deep breath and stepped onto the board and knelt down. The record was for the highest stand-up paddle, not the highest kneel-down paddle, so as long as I didn't stand up and paddle the record was Maya's.

The board wasn't pumped up enough to hold my weight, so it bowed a bit in the middle. Water came over the board and wet my pants and boots. I thought, *I'll deal with that later.*

I pushed off and slowly paddled out into the middle of the lake. As I looked down at the paddle, I could see a build-up of ice on the blade every time I put it in the water. I couldn't work out why the paddle was freezing but the lake wasn't. Apparently, that's down to glacier bloom, where sediment from the glacier in the water gives it a unique colour and unusual freezing properties. I knew that meant that, if Maya fell in, she'd be covered in ice.

I kept paddling and turned around to face the team, who were now about 30 metres away. I remembered Lewis Pugh talking about the lake only being a metre deep, so I put my paddle down into the water vertically . . . and it went down and down and down. *It's got to stop!* I thought. But it didn't. It was a two-metre paddle and it didn't touch the bottom of the lake. That meant the water would be well over both of our heads.

Slowly I paddled back to shore. I was really nervous at the thought of Maya actually standing up and paddling. When I looked over at her, she was completely amped.

I pulled up alongside the rock, hopped off the board and handed the paddle to Maya. There was a bit of thin ice around the edge of the lake and I pointed it out to her. She just wanted to get on the board as soon as possible.

Ben lay down and held one end of the board, and Maya carefully knelt on it. I made a mental note that a rescue line was just behind me. She sat up on her knees and I handed her the paddle. Then it was time.

'OK, Maya, push off.'

She floated out, clear of the shore ice. My heart was in my mouth.

'OK, Maya, stand up carefully and start paddling slowly . . .'

She sprang up onto her feet and started to paddle. Everyone around clapped and cheered.

She had done it! The highest stand-up paddleboard ever on the planet—and she was only 12 years old.

I took a brief moment to look around and take everything in. It was so cool that Maya had set this goal and achieved it. The chance of failing was huge, but that hadn't stopped her; in fact, it had motivated her even more.

Maya slowly paddled back to shore. I held out my hand as she hopped onto the rock, dry as a bone and with a huge smile from ear to ear. Everyone congratulated her, and she was so happy.

We took a few moments to celebrate, before our thoughts turned to getting back down to Gorak Shep. The team got onto deflating the board, while I took Maya into the tent and helped her get the wetsuit off—a struggle at sea level, let alone at 5000 metres! She managed to get it off fine and I left her in the tent to get dressed.

Moments after she came out of the tent, the Sherpa had it packed down. Nawang gave Maya a mug of hot sweet tea and a bag of trusty popcorn. She was still smiling.

A few minutes later, we were all trekking back up the ridge—and my nerves started to jangle just thinking of having to get back down across the moraine.

I asked Nawang if two Sherpa could hang back with us, in case we had to piggyback Maya. I was worried that she was going to crash as she was on a massive adrenaline buzz and she'd spent so much energy.

As we started up the hill, Maya's energy levels came crashing down. 'Dad, I'm really tired.'

'I know, Maya. Just go slowly to the top of the ridge and we will rest.'

Determined, she carried on.

We stopped for a break at the top of the ridge. This turned out to be a bit of a mistake as, from there, we could see all of the ridges we had to cross to get back to Gorak Shep. The light was starting to fade, and I was worried.

Needlessly worried, as it turned out, because as soon as we got up and started downhill Maya perked up and didn't have another problem.

When we got to the top of the last ridge, I gave Nawang my pack and Maya hopped on my back—a good old Dad piggyback at over 5000 metres!

I lasted all of about five minutes before I had to put Maya down. Nawang motioned to me to take the packs, then he piggybacked her. He lasted 15 minutes, so my effort was just a token!

With a kilometre to go across the flat of the dry lakebed, Nawang decided to hurry back so he could organise dinner. It was perfect timing, as it left Maya and me to cruise in together. I piggybacked her some more of the way, but after about seven minutes my lungs started screaming, so from there on we just walked together.

When we walked into the tea house, the whole team was there and greeted Maya with applause. She thanked them, then sat down to play cards as if nothing had happened.

I was so proud of her, but she didn't really think anything of it. It was just what we did. She was passionate about this adventure and really wanted to achieve it, so she did. Having that passion was really important as it helped motivate her and keep her on track when the going got tough.

After dinner, Nawang, Maya and I were sitting in my room talking when I got called away. When I returned, I found Maya sitting there with an oxygen mask over her face.

I panicked. I'd only been gone a few minutes. What could possibly have gone wrong?

'Oh my god! Are you OK?'

She held her phone out to take a selfie. 'Yeah, yeah, Dad. Just sending Mum a photo . . . without any caption.' She grinned.

I felt my heart rate slowing. 'Are you sure that's a wise idea?' I asked gently.

Maya thought about it for a minute. 'Yeah, good point,' she said. 'Mum would probably freak out.'

You've got to be kidding me! I thought.

Meanwhile, Nawang was sitting in the corner, chuckling.

While the oxygen had provided Maya with a little joke, later that night I was very glad we had it. At around 2am, there was a knock on my door. It was one of the guys from the trekking team. He said his partner wasn't well and he was really worried about her.

The first thing I did was find Nawang. He sprang into action and, with the emergency oxygen in hand, we went up to the clients' room. I quickly realised she was doing what's known as Cheyne-Stokes breathing. This is where your breathing gets into a really abnormal pattern, getting progressively deeper and slower until you temporarily stop breathing altogether and start gasping for air.

It's all to do with breathing triggers, which are usually regulated by carbon dioxide build-up in the blood stream, but at altitude the carbon dioxide levels are all stuffed up because you breathe faster. The body is very clever and it falls back on another trigger to breathe—lack of oxygen to the brain—which results in breathing stopping for a little bit followed by a huge gasp for air. When I was on Everest I had a Cheyne-Stokes breathing episode, so I knew how terrifying it could be.

Altitude doesn't care who you are, how tough you think you are or how much experience you have.

Nawang instantly put the oxygen mask on the client, while I went and woke Ben. After a quick check-up, he assured her she would be fine and left her on oxygen for the night. Sure enough, in the morning she was a box of birds.

The whole episode just proved to me the importance of

having emergency oxygen readily available. All the top-quality Everest base camp treks do the same. If you are planning to do a trek to Everest base camp, take it seriously, as the consequences can be unthinkable. Altitude doesn't care who you are, how tough you think you are or how much experience you have, so don't do it on the cheap—go with a good company, as you really get what you pay for with trekking in Nepal.

▲

The next day was going to be a long one, as we planned to get all the way back down to Pangboche. Usually, I stop at Lobuche for a night, so I was a little nervous to see how it was going to go.

The trek down from Everest base camp is awesome, because with every step down you feel better. As you get lower, you can feel the air becoming thicker. It's quite weird, but I love it. Thankfully, everyone handled the seven-hour walk back to Gurman's lodge quite easily—perhaps because of the promise of roast chicken and a hot shower at the end of it.

The following day, I decided to take a bit of a diversion on the way back to Namche Bazaar. Instead of following the direct route, we went through Phortse. It was a spectacular trek. Maya and I walked together. When we stopped at the top of one hill for a drink of water and some popcorn, I heard a low-pitched 'Whoosh!' and looked up to see two huge Himalayan eagles flying about 15 metres above our heads. It was an incredible sight. We sat for ages as they circled on the thermals, gaining altitude. Just magic.

Phortse is a really traditional village and arriving there

feels a little bit like being in a time warp with the stone homes, and the farmers tending their vegetable crops and looking after their yaks.

Shortly after we arrived, I heard a yak squawking away. It sounded distressed. I looked towards the source of the noise to see Nawang showing Maya a baby yak. Wherever this baby's mother was, I knew she would not be impressed by this.

'NAWANG! What are you doing?' I screeched.

Nawang laughed. 'I'm showing Maya a baby yak.'

'What about the mother?' I said, panicking.

Nawang giggled and shrugged. 'Not sure where she is.'

The baby yak continued to bleat away. Maya gave it a pat, then Nawang let it go. All with no sign of Mama Yak, thank goodness. She would have charged us if she'd seen or heard what we were doing.

After lunch at Pemba's parents' tea house, we trekked down, down, down to the river, and then back up the other side. It's a hard, two-hour walk up but the magnificent views make it all worthwhile.

Back at Namaste Lodge, we all enjoyed Palden and Tsering's characteristic outstanding hospitality. After dinner, the rest of the team went off to the pub, while Maya and I stayed and played cards with Palden.

Also staying that night was my friend Thundu Sherpa. I first met Thundu when we climbed Ama Dablam together, and he'd been on Everest with me as well. We'd kept in touch over the years, and it was great to have the chance to catch up with him.

Thundu had a real presence about him, a real sense of mana. He was very quiet, but he laughed a lot. He was on his way up to climb Ama Dablam with some clients.

He asked me to go to the pub with him that evening, but I

had already told Maya I would stay with her at Palden's. As he left, Thundu shook my hand and pulled me in for a hug, saying, 'OK, Mike-dai, take care. See you later.' (*Dai* means brother in Sherpa.) Now I wish so much that I had gone out with him, but I wasn't to know that it was the last time I would ever see him. A few weeks later, Thundu was hit on the head by a falling rock on Dablam. Despite wearing a helmet, his injuries were fatal.

▲

There was a bit of excitement at the lodge the next morning as Palden had organised a scenic helicopter flight for the team up to Everest base camp and back down to Lukla. About half of the team had decided to do it, and Maya and I got to go along for the ride.

While the rest of the team left to walk back down to Lukla, we sat and waited at the helicopter pad. And waited . . . and waited . . . and waited. There was no sign of the helicopter all morning.

By midday, I came up with a plan B for the day. As it was about a nine-hour walk to Lukla, there was no way we could get ourselves back down there by nightfall. I decided we'd head for Phakding for the night, then get up before dawn and trek in the dark to catch the flight from Lukla the following day. The big question was how long we should continue to sit there and wait for the helicopter.

That decision was taken out of my hands when finally a chopper came into view in the distance. The noise got louder and the chopper got bigger. Yep, it was definitely heading our way.

Maya and I hid behind a big rock as it came into land. I've been paranoid about watching helicopters land ever since a friend of mine told me that he'd been watching a huge Russian helicopter land at base camp and it crashed right in front of his eyes. He saw it beat itself into pieces. A chunk of tail rotor flew towards him and hit the ground about 30 centimetres away, penetrating the earth as it landed. Since then, I try to avoid being near helicopters that are landing out in the wild.

The chopper had to make three trips to get all of us down to Lukla. Maya and I were on the last one, and it was so cool to fly over all the places we'd just been. We saw the lake that Maya had set her world record on—it looked so isolated, like the end of the world. Then we flew past Ama Dablam—it's so beautiful, but so deadly. We flew back down past Namche Bazaar, and a few minutes later we were in Lukla. We hopped off the chopper and there was a lot of noise and wind as it took off and headed back up the Everest valley.

It was a weird feeling, standing there in Lukla. One moment, we'd been trekking at Namche and the next we were in Lukla, ready to go home. I guess my brain was used to processing the trip home while I walked back to Lukla, but this time it didn't have the chance.

After a night at Paradise Lodge with Dawa, we flew back to Kathmandu. When we got to Hotel Manaslu, Maya hopped on her Instagram account for the first time in a while. She had posted a photo of herself at Everest base camp on my shoulders. This was the first time she got to read the comments. They were all super supportive.

'Amazing, Maya!'

'Well done!'

'Brilliant.'

▲

When Maya and I landed back in Auckland, Wendy, Ethan and Dylan were there to meet us. There was a lot of hugging. Maya talked about the trip and the boys asked heaps of questions about base camp and paddleboarding on the lake.

That night at dinner, Ethan seemed a bit more interested in asking me about Kilimanjaro than about Nepal. While we'd been away, he'd decided on what his 14-year-old adventure was going to be—and I was excited to help him plan for it. In the meantime, we had Christmas and the summer holidays to think about.

While we'd been away, Ethan had decided on what his 14-year-old adventure was going to be—and I was excited to help him plan for it.

Wendy and I spent New Year's Eve with a bottle of nice champagne, just letting our dreams flow, as we do every year. Wendy said she didn't want to do any full-on adventures that year. Instead, she wanted to go to Europe and visit her brother in the UK. So that was the plan. The cool thing about each person sharing their dreams and goals is it opens up so many more ideas. Besides which, I can find adventure anywhere!

Wendy and I want to make the most of the time we have with our family while the kids are still young. Time flies by so fast that building awesome memories and traditions with them is our priority. Plus a trip to Europe was something that Wendy really wanted to do and I wanted her to be happy— because if Mum and Dad are OK then the family is OK.

▲

Back at school, Maya wrote her speech and I helped her practise it over and over. On the day she was a bit nervous, but she did really well. All the other students seemed very interested in her adventure. I was there too, and we did a question-and-answer segment on stage. Maya was brilliant at answering everything.

Months passed and the family was back in the full swing of normal life. School, weekend sports, work—just the usual.

Nawang emailed me and sent me some photos showing a new roof on one of the widow's houses. Both Maya and I were chuffed, as the fundraising had worked just as we'd wanted it to.

In August, we departed for Europe with the kids. After catching up with BJ in London, we went to Spain, where we stayed at a friend's house for a week. It was amazing and I fell completely in love with that country.

One afternoon, we were sitting in a plaza on the Costa Brava. Wendy had a glass of rosé and I had a local beer. We had just finished lunch and the kids wanted to go and get an ice cream from a shop across the plaza. I had one rule: you want something, you have to ask for it in Spanish yourself.

The kids did paper, scissors, rock to decide who was going to go and attempt to speak Spanish. Ethan lost. Then they all got on Google Translate and Ethan practised asking for 'three ice creams, please'.

Soon they were back with three huge ice creams and three even bigger smiles.

Ethan said, 'We asked him in Spanish, Dad, and he said he could speak English, so we spoke English!'

It was worth a try.

CHAPTER 20

LAMA GESHE

One morning in February 2018, I got a message from one of my friends in Pangboche. 'We've lost our Lama Geshe, Mike. Lama Geshe has passed away.'

That message was followed by many more from my Sherpa friends who knew how important Lama Geshe had been to me and my family. I sat and looked at the photograph hanging on our wall of Lama Geshe blessing Maya. I just felt so sad. He was a bigger part of our family that we even really realised.

When I told Wendy what had happened, she said I should go to Nepal to attend Lama Geshe's puja ceremonies. It felt like the right thing to do, and I was due to go on leave in a week's time. I called my manager, explained what had happened and asked if I could take some extra time off. My boss was great and quickly sorted out my leave, removing me from a week's worth of duties on compassionate grounds.

With that sorted, I arranged a flight to Singapore through work then got online and booked myself the next available cheap(ish) flight to Kathmandu. It was leaving that night, so it was a bit of a rush to get organised.

That afternoon, I picked Maya up from school so I could tell her about Lama Geshe myself before she found out on social media. She was sad and asked a few questions about what had happened to him. When we got home, the boys were there and I told them too. The kids could see I was very sad about Lama Geshe, and they gave me lots of hugs.

The whole family came out to the airport to see me off. I would be gone for three weeks.

▲

When I got to Kathmandu, Rajan was there waiting for me. It was nice to see him again, and to be back in Nepal. He took me to Hotel Manaslu, where I was staying the night.

It soon became obvious that there was no way any fixed-wing aircraft would be getting in or out of there today.

The next morning, the weather was bad in Lukla, but Rajan had organised a seat on a helicopter for me. He'd even sorted out cashing in my airline ticket, so all I had to do was pay an extra US$100 and I was away.

We flew low up a valley to Lukla, and it soon became obvious that there was no way any fixed-wing aircraft would be getting in or out of there today, as the cloud was very low. Thank goodness for Rajan arranging the chopper, as I couldn't lose a single day if I was to make it to Pangboche in time.

Dawa was surprised to see me walking in the door at Paradise Lodge. She made me some breakfast, before putting a silk scarf around my neck and wishing me luck.

I walked up to Monjo that day, and it was beautiful to be on my own. It gave me time to think. When I got to Namche the following day, Palden wasn't there, as it was still winter so trekking season hadn't yet begun. Pretty much nothing is open in winter, which had the potential to make my trek slightly tricky.

Thankfully, I found one lodge that was open in Namche and I spent the night there. It was so strange not being at Palden's. It was even stranger to be the only person staying at the lodge.

There were a few trekkers on the trail, but not many. The ones I had spoken to had been tricked into trekking by irresponsible companies. They'd arrived expecting the classic Nepal trekking experience only to find nearly everything closed, including Gorak Shep, the village just before base camp.

From Namche, I trekked all the way up to Pangboche. Rushing up to altitude that fast is not recommended and I knew I was going to get a headache.

Walking into the village was emotional. Pangboche is so beautiful with its terraced fields and traditional houses, but there's also a tinge of sadness as every family has lost relatives to Everest and the Himalaya.

I went straight to Gurman's house and he greeted me

warmly. I walked into his dining room, where three young Sherpa were making up packages of food and sweets for a puja. These would then be blessed and distributed to everyone in the village. Gurman explained that they were for his mother's second puja ceremony. She had passed away 45 days ago. The Sherpa perform two puja ceremonies when someone dies. The first is when the person is cremated and the second is 45 days after their death, as this is the length of time they believe Buddha meditated under a sacred tree.

I had some tea and soup with Gurman before I headed up to Lama Geshe's house. I could feel the tears welling up in my eyes as I left, and I hoped I would be OK once I got to his house.

It's about a 20-minute walk to Upper Pangboche. As soon as I saw Lama Geshe's house, I started thinking about all the times I'd visited him over the last 15 years. I thought about the impact he'd had on me, my family and on my trekking clients.

As I got to his front door, I could see that the house was a hive of activity. A huge tent had been put up outside to accommodate all the visitors. A Sherpa woman in beautiful traditional dress gave me tea and welcomed me.

One of the first people I saw was Nawang's brother, Kusang. He gave me a big hug and told me to wait in the tent while he went to find Lama Geshe's son, Jigmi, who had flown in from his home in the United States.

Kusang appeared with Jigmi, who I had met a few years before. Jigmi shook my hand, and I started to speak. 'I'm so sorry for your loss. I've come to pay my respects—'

I barely got the words out before I burst into tears and was unable to continue talking. I just put my head down and stood there. Jigmi patted me on the back and said, 'It's

OK, Mike. I know how much he meant to you. Thank you for coming all this way.'

Jigmi then led me inside the house. He stopped at the dining-room door and said, 'Mike, my father is in this room. He is embalmed and the lamas are saying prayers starting in a few minutes. Please go in and put your prayer scarf in front of him, then kneel before him and walk clockwise around him, OK?'

I nodded then I walked into the room.

Lama Geshe's body was sitting upright in a chair, all wrapped up and decorated with so many colourful Buddhist prayer flags. There were numerous golden statues of Buddha surrounding him.

I placed a silk scarf on a pile of other scarves, along with my donation to the family. I then knelt down and touched the floor with my head. I stood up again, touching my head, mouth and heart with my hands. I repeated this three times as Jigmi had instructed, then I walked clockwise around Lama Geshe.

Jigmi then told me to sit down, as this was my time to say goodbye to his father. 'We believe that my father can hear you. This is where you say goodbye and talk to him. He can hear you.'

Well, that just made me cry even more. I sat there and told Lama Geshe what he meant to me, and I thanked him for blessing me and my family, for keeping me safe in the mountains, especially on Everest, for naming my children and for opening my eyes to the gift of giving unconditionally to others, for making me understand the importance of giving more than I take in this world and for passing that on to my children.

Soon all the lamas and monks came back into the room for the next round of prayers. I got up to leave, but Jigmi asked me to stay.

Buddhist monks sat on either side of me. There were 29 of them in the room, and me there right in the middle. They started a deep, guttural chanting as they repeated their prayers over and over. Some of them played horns, trumpets, cymbals and a drum. The noise was deafening. They played and prayed, while I just sat there and soaked it all in. It was incredibly healing.

Then they chanted a prayer that I recognised—it was the same one Lama Geshe blessed me with before I climbed Everest. The tears just flowed.

The prayer session lasted 90 minutes, but it felt like no time had passed at all.

When I went to leave, Jigmi stopped me and invited me to stay for lunch. He brought out a beautiful vegetable curry and some rather potent rice wine.

The monks all acknowledged me and smiled. One of them recognised me, having seen me in the village before. He said, 'You're the New Zealand pilot.'

I smiled and said yes. He replied very sincerely, 'Thank you for coming.'

After lunch, Jigmi asked me to be at the house at seven the following morning. 'We will feed you and then we will carry my father up into the mountains, where we will cremate him. See you tomorrow.'

I thanked him and started walking back down to Gurman's. I took the upper track and stopped along the way. There was no one around at all. I just sat there and soaked up the view down to Pangboche.

I was the only one staying at Sonam Lodge with Gurman, his wife and their daughter. We had more vegetable curry for dinner, then I headed to bed. I'd never been in the Himalaya in winter before, and it was absolutely freezing.

In the morning, I woke up with a frozen water bottle and frozen condensation on the windows. I scraped the crusted icicles off the window and looked at the view. There was Ama Dablam, towering over me. I lay back on the pillow and just stared at the mountain as the dawn light reflected off it. I could see where I had climbed all those years ago.

I got dressed and slowly walked to Upper Pangboche. There were a few other people walking up towards Lama Geshe's house as well.

When I got there, I was greeted by a Sherpa woman who gave me a bowl of porridge and a cup of sweet Sherpa tea. There was a lot of activity both inside and outside the house. I think every single person from the village was there and they were all wearing traditional Sherpa dress. The men were all in black and had cowboy hats on. I'm not sure how these became part of Sherpa culture, but they are. There were Buddhist monks dressed in red wearing hats with what looked like a Mohawk sticking up out of them. Many were carrying musical instruments—there were lots of drums, horns of varying sizes and cymbals.

I felt like all of my senses were in overload from the sounds, the sights and the smells. It was like nothing I could have imagined.

People were jostling into different positions, and there were bundles of incense burning everywhere. One of the

Sherpa women gave me a bundle and lit it for me. There were also juniper bushes being burned everywhere. I felt like all of my senses were in overload from the sounds, the sights and the smells. It was like nothing I could have imagined.

Then Lama Geshe was brought out, still sitting upright, and decorated with prayer flags and silk scarves.

The entire village was there. Lama Geshe had meant so much to every one of us. The women were all standing together weeping, and the small children with them were crying as well. The men stood over on the steps leading up towards the mountains. They all looked sad, but none of them shed any tears.

The trumpets began to play, and the monks started chanting to the sound of the beating drums. It was time for the procession to make its way up the side of the mountain. Twelve strong Sherpa carried Lama Geshe on his throne up the stairs and along a track up the mountain.

The men went first, along with Lama Geshe, and the women followed behind. I ended up trailing behind the men to the point where the women nearly caught up with me. One of the Sherpa women grabbed my hand and pulled me up a steep bit of the track, then pushed me towards the men. She did it in a caring, gentle way. It was clear to me that she felt I was supposed to be with the men. To tell the truth, I was struggling with the altitude and was having trouble keeping up.

I could tell that a lot of people were talking about me and the fact that I had come from New Zealand to pay my respects. I felt not only welcomed but also very privileged to be accepted.

After about 20 minutes' walking, the funeral procession

arrived at the cremation site. I was really worried about watching the cremation, as I've seen some Hindu cremations and they can be confronting for a Westerner. The fire roars away while the family gathers around and watches their loved one being cremated in front of them. I've even seen body parts fall out of the fire and the family members casually pick them up and put them back into the fire. It looks brutal to a foreigner, but I had to keep reminding myself that it's their tradition.

A long queue formed and I joined it to say my final farewell. Everyone shuffled past Lama Geshe, bowing as they got to him and placing a silk scarf on him.

As I moved around the cremation chamber, I was relieved to see it was fully enclosed. It looked like a three-metre-high egg made out of rock, cement and plaster. There was an opening on one side, through which Lama Geshe was placed inside on top of a pile of wood. Next to the opening, there was a pile of stones ready to seal the chamber up once it had been set alight.

Once the farewells were finished, everyone sat down. There were about 200 people there—young and old, men, women, children, monks and lamas—all sitting on a steep slope above a cremation chamber on the side of a mountain in the Himalaya. It was only then that I realised I was the only Westerner there. It had been some of that momentary courage that had made me decide to get on a plane and come. That and Wendy's support and encouragement. I felt so privileged to be sitting there in that moment.

After a short time, Kusang came and took me down to the cremation chamber. He told me to sit with the monks and lamas. Everyone had some tea, then lunch was served—a beautiful curry and pickled vegetables—and someone came around and poured cups of rice wine. Man, it was strong.

Smoke started drifting slowly around us as the fire was lit, while everyone sat eating their lunch and quietly showing respect.

The fire roared away, consuming Lama Geshe's body. Stonemasons quickly built a wall with rocks to seal the chamber so no one could see inside it. Prayers and mantras were continuously chanted, while traditional musical instruments were played. It was very sad, but also very healing.

Then, right at the best possible moment, someone pointed to the sky. Five huge Himalayan golden eagles were circling overhead, around and around.

Then, right at the best possible moment, someone pointed to the sky. Five huge Himalayan golden eagles were circling overhead, around and around. Soon the entire crowd was looking up at the sky. The eagles were extremely significant. If an eagle appears at a cremation ceremony, the Sherpa believe that they are taking the person's spirit and soul on to their next life. To see five of them was amazing.

As I sat there drinking my rice wine, my head spinning a little, someone cleared my plate and another person offered me some dessert. Then a line of nine people formed and started moving past everyone. They were all handing out money. When they got to me, the first of them tried to give me 100 rupees. I was confused and said, 'Thank you, but I'm OK. Please give this to someone else.'

Jigmi was one of the people handing out money, and he spoke to me quietly. 'Mike, it is our tradition. We now pay everyone on the mountain. Please, you must take it.'

I sat there and was handed more and more money. I ended up with 900 rupees (NZ$11). I put this in my pocket to give to the porters on the trek out the next day.

After a few more hours, people slowly started dispersing and returning to their homes and their lives. I returned to Sonam for the night.

▲

In the morning, I went up to see Jigmi to thank him for making me feel so welcome, then I set off back to Namche.

Along the way, I meet up with a lama. He was dressed in red and spoke English. His name was Lama Tenzing. He said, 'My friend, I saw you at Lama Geshe's puja. He was my mentor and my friend, too.'

I told him what Lama Geshe had meant to me and my family, and how he had named my kids. Lama Tenzing told me his monastery was in Khunde, just over the hill from Ed Hillary's school at Khumjung, and invited me to come to his home, but sadly I didn't have time.

I asked him if I could bring my teams to him for a blessing each year. He said he would be delighted to help us.

We trekked together for a bit and I felt a real connection with him. Lama Tenzing had a presence about him that was similar to Lama Geshe. It was really strange, almost as if Lama Geshe was watching over us and had introduced us. We bid each other goodbye, and I carried on to Namche, knowing I would see Lama Tenzing again.

CHAPTER 21

ETHAN'S KILIMANJARO

I n the year-and-a-bit since Maya and I had come back from her paddleboarding adventure, Ethan had been busy planning his own 14-year-old trip with Dad. He had his heart set on climbing Mount Kilimanjaro with me.

Here's the kicker, though. Maya had set an unofficial world record—unofficial because we hadn't got the Guinness World Record people involved, and Maya was happy with that as she reckons that anyone who searches online will find her record. However, Maya's record led Ethan to decide he wanted to set an *official* one, recognised by the Guinness Book of World Records. He spent quite a bit of time researching and trying to work out what he could do that would earn him that record while we were on Kilimanjaro.

While he was coming up with ideas, I had to remind him

of the rules of this new tradition: it had to be outside what he thought was possible so it would push his limits, it had to be safe and have Wendy's approval, and it had to give back to others in some way.

Eventually, he came up with an idea. He was going to carry a board game to the summit of Kilimanjaro and there he would play the world's highest board game. He'd worked out that, if he got any publicity as a result of the attempt, he'd use that to help raise money for charity.

Ethan thought about a game of chess and did some research, however there were already two climbers who had played a game of chess at 8000 metres in the Himalaya, so that record was gone. He then thought about playing a game of chess with a twist—challenge a grand master to a game over the internet, with the grand master at sea level and Ethan at the summit of Mount Kilimanjaro.

Ethan and I wrote an email to a grand master called Jan Gustafsson in Germany. He has an amazing app called Chess24, where you can challenge people from all around the world to play games online. Jan replied straight away, but there was a technical issue. A person can't challenge other users or accept challenges. The app is entirely random in who plays who. So that idea didn't work out, but it was a good lesson in reaching out to people for help.

Instead, Ethan decided he would play the world's highest game of Guess Who?

▲

With a goal in place, it was time to start planning. Ethan decided that he wanted to use the adventure to raise money for Auckland City Mission, and thereby help the homeless here in Auckland. He set up a fundraising page and let everyone on his social media know what he was hoping to achieve.

I wasn't sure how he'd cope with talking to people about the trip, as sometimes it was a struggle to get him to say more than a few words at a time. A typical teenager, he was a bit shy about the whole thing, but he realised that he needed to talk to people to raise awareness for his fundraising.

Ethan was a bit shy about the whole thing, but he realised that he needed to talk to people to raise awareness for his fundraising.

When it came to sorting out the Kilimanjaro side of things, I was lucky that I'd been there before. The company I'd gone with in 2001, Zara Tours, was still operating so I got in touch with them and they sorted out everything on the ground there. That included porters, guides, rental gear, tents, food—heck, they were even going to pick us up at the airport. I knew they'd do a good job for us and there was the added bonus that their prices were really reasonable.

Then came the flights. There's no straightforward way to get from Auckland to Kilimanjaro International Airport in Tanzania. We looked at heaps of different options, but eventually decided to head to London, where we could stay with BJ. From there we booked flights on Ethiopian Airlines to Kilimanjaro, with a brief stop in Addis Ababa.

▲

As usual, the day we left Auckland was a mad rush of last-minute packing, gear checking, passport checking, gear rechecking . . . as well as a quick interview for a TV news show about our planned mission.

Ethan was great on TV, if a bit of a teenager—he didn't say much and the reporter had to squeeze answers out of him. At one stage, he picked up a sleeping mat and said, 'This is a sleeping mat for sleeping on . . .' Classic. I admit I teased him a bit on that one.

When the interview was screened, they described Ethan as 'Mountain Boy'. It seemed like all of his friends paused their TVs and took a photo of the Mountain Boy caption so they could text it to him and give him a hard time. Ethan took it all in his stride, as it was good-natured ribbing.

Once that was all done, Wendy, Maya and Dylan waved goodbye to us at the airport and we were off on our adventure.

When we landed in Los Angeles 14 hours later, Ethan could barely wait for the flight attendant to say, 'Welcome to Los Angeles. The local time is 11am. You are welcome to turn your devices on,' before he had his phone out.

He wasn't hanging out to get on social media, though; he wanted to check his Givealittle page to see if anyone had made donations to his charity as a result of the news coverage. His phone beeped repeatedly when he switched it on, each tone signifying another donation. He was stoked.

After a couple of days hanging out at BJ's place in London, it was time to get down to the business at hand. We both packed our gear and made sure that the hopefully soon to be world-record-earning edition of Guess Who? was carefully wrapped.

I hadn't flown with Ethiopian Airlines before, and I found

them absolutely fantastic. Check-in was smooth, the A350 Airbus was brand new, the crew were friendly, the meals were really tasty and the inflight entertainment was state of the art. The flight through to Addis Ababa was just under eight hours and I couldn't fault a thing on it.

In Addis, we had to change planes for our onward flight to Kilimanjaro. While we waited, we grabbed some food and hung out in the terminal. I was expecting a small plane for the two-hour hop to Kilimanjaro, but it was another brand-new A350—and the flight was packed.

About an hour into the flight, Mount Kilimanjaro came into view, towering through the clouds. It's a wide mountain and it had heaps of snow on it. I'd never seen it with that much snow before, not even in photos. Ethan was shocked by just how big it looked. 'Holy smoke, Dad. It's massive.'

At Kilimanjaro Airport, we were met by border officers who were asking to see proof that passengers had been vaccinated against yellow fever. I hadn't been expecting this, but apparently people coming from countries with a known risk for the disease are legally required to have been vaccinated before entering Tanzania. There's a good reason for this, as the disease can be fatal. It is spread by mosquitoes and about 50 per cent of people who contract it develop serious symptoms, including bleeding, shock and organ failure causing death.

New Zealand, the United States and the United Kingdom don't have yellow fever, but Ethiopia does, so apparently we needed to have had the vaccination. I'm not sure how we would have been infected in the short time we spent at the airport in Addis, as the disease is usually carried by mosquitoes and the city is too high and too dry for them to survive, but there you go.

We were given the option of an on-the-spot vaccination for US$250 each. Not for the first time during our travels, I was really grateful to know Dr Marc Shaw. He's our travel doctor, and he knows all about travelling in African countries and how requirements there can change quickly. He'd given Ethan and me our yellow fever shots along with a whole lot of other vaccinations before we left Auckland.

We flashed our yellow fever vaccination certificates and carried on to the customs queue. Seconds later, a Zara Tours representative introduced herself to us. I couldn't work out how she knew who we were, but she laughed and reminded me that we'd sent the company photographs of ourselves as part of the booking process. Smart!

She then took our passports and the money for our visas and disappeared. With nothing else to do, Ethan and I sat down and watched a huge queue of passengers form in front of just two customs desks. They were in for a long wait.

A couple of minutes later, our guide returned. She'd managed to work some magic and secure our visas for Tanzania without us having to queue. I was stoked.

Once we'd chucked our bags through the final X-ray check, we headed outside to where a Land Rover was waiting for us. While I was sorting our luggage out, I got chatting to an American guy called Marcon. He was organising some climbing clients, and told me that he'd summited Kilimanjaro about 50 times. That's impressive. He said he was staying at the same hotel as us, so I hoped to catch up with him later for a drink. I was really curious to find out how he managed to guide on the mountain when it was so highly regulated.

When Ethan and I got into the car, he said, 'Dad, why didn't you tell him that you had climbed Everest?'

I laughed and said, 'Sometimes it's best just to keep things to yourself.'

The drive to Springlands Hotel took about 40 minutes from the airport and along the way we could see Masai herdsmen looking after their animals. They were very tall, dressed in traditional red and carrying long staffs.

As we drove through the town of Moshi, I couldn't help but notice the changes that had happened since I was last there. In 2001, it was all dirt roads with huge potholes; now it was all sealed. I guess that's what comes with being on the route to a mountain that's on every climber's bucket list.

As we passed a football ground, we saw hundreds of people dancing in lines. African drums were being played really loud and all these people were jumping up and down in tune to them. It was absolutely amazing. Ethan looked a bit overwhelmed, but he is really sharp and spotted the hotel the instant it came into view. It reminded me of India when he was seven and he'd spotted our hotel sign next to the rubble.

Arriving at the hotel, my memories of my previous stay came flooding back. It's set amongst beautiful gardens with fishponds, a restaurant and a pool. Ethan was pretty excited to finally be there.

I was a little bit spooked when we got to our room and I found out it was the exact same one I'd stayed in last time. I decided that had to be a good omen!

After a quick lunch, we went over to the gear rental room—seriously, this place had everything!—to pick up a couple of things I'd forgotten. The key thing was gaiters to go over our boots. These are essential on Kilimanjaro as there is a lot of scree near the summit and getting small stones in your boots up there is a real pain.

From there, we headed to the garden to meet our guide, Mndeme, for a briefing. We sat at the same table I'd sat at 17 years ago and were given the same briefing. Amazing.

The great thing about doing a one-on-one adventure with a teenager is that it's a real chance to bond, to talk and to work as a team. It was a completely different dynamic to when we were at home.

We also met the two other people who were going to be climbing with us—cousins from Chennai in India called Prajod and Prasanna.

With the briefing complete and our gear organised, Ethan and I spent the evening sitting in the garden-bar area talking. The great thing about doing a one-on-one adventure with a teenager is that it's a real chance to bond, to talk and to work as a team. It was a completely different dynamic to when we were at home. Here, on adventure, there was no such thing as a moody teenager. I need to get a patent on this—if you have a moody, one-word-answer, grunting teen, take them on an adventure!

While we were sitting there, Marcon stopped by for a chat. We talked about climbing for a while and shared stories about our climbing adventures and our experiences as trek leaders. I mentioned my Everest summit and base camp trips when the time felt right. Then Marcon had to go off to do something for one of his clients.

About 15 minutes later, he came back. He walked straight up to me and said, 'Mike, I've been thinking, and I'm going to help you start a guiding business on Kilimanjaro. I'll introduce you to Zara from Zara Tours, and I'll do everything in my power to help you.'

I was blown away.

He carried on, saying, 'I'm looking at retiring and it would be nice to help someone like you who would enjoy guiding teams on Kilimanjaro.'

This was a dream come true!

After Marcon left, Ethan said, 'Dad, that is awesome. Can I help you guide when you run your trips?'

'We will see . . .' I said.

While Ethan and I were having dinner, Marcon came over to talk to us again. This time he had a woman with him. She had this real presence about her and I knew she had to be important. Then Marcon introduced us. It was only Zara herself!

We chatted for a few minutes, but she had to go and meet someone else. She suggested that we set up a meeting when I got back from the climb. I eagerly agreed, somewhat surprised by this unusual turn of events.

As Ethan and I got ready for bed, I could feel my nerves kick in. It happens before every adventure out in the unknown. And this was the unknown—I didn't know how the week was going to end. I didn't know if we'd make the summit. I didn't know if Ethan would be OK. I didn't know if the weather was going to be OK. Would there be too much snow? Should I have got crampons? Would I get sick? Would Ethan get sick? It was an exciting time, but I had to try hard not to be overwhelmed by all these questions and concerns.

Whenever I start to feel overwhelmed, I try to focus on being in the moment and I think about the things I do know. There, in Kilimanjaro with my son, it was no different.

I just focused on the moment and soon that feeling of being overwhelmed disappeared and left me clear-headed enough to think about other stuff.

▲

The following morning, we sat and waited at the main gate while Mndeme did all the paperwork. There was plenty of activity to keep us occupied while we waited—porters weighing gear and guides organising teams. There was a tiny issue with Ethan being a bit young, but it soon got smoothed out. Things seemed a lot more organised than they had been when I was last there.

Before long, our little team of four was joined by 12 porters, two assistant guides and a head guide. It seemed like a lot of people, but the rules are very clear: each porter is allowed to carry a maximum of 15 kilograms, there are to be three porters per climber, and each party has to have at least one guide and one assistant guide.

That might seem excessive, but I thought it was great as the national park, who set the rules, were clearly looking after the well-being of the guides and porters, and at the same time creating jobs for the community. Imagine if they could do the same in Nepal.

After an hour of waiting, it was time to get moving. We walked up to the gate, where two armed guards with AK47s were shouting at people. It turned out that there was nothing to worry about, though, and minutes later we were through the gate and on our way.

It wasn't long before I started to hear the word 'polepole' frequently. It took me right back to being in Nepal with

Nawang! He'd been right—it is the Swahili word for slow.

The track starts off as a tarsealed road, then turns into a dirt road, then becomes a smaller track leading into the jungle. The noise in the jungle was amazing. The birds were raucously loud and I loved hearing the monkeys calling from high in the tree canopy.

The first day's hiking covered 18 kilometres up a gradual incline. Ethan and I walked by ourselves for most of the day, although we were sometimes joined by one of the assistant guides called Salimu. The conversation was great and sometimes there was just silence—we didn't need to talk to each other but were still connected, all without having to do times tables out loud this time.

Soon enough, we arrived at the Machame camp and saw our tents for the first time. They were huge for two people. In Nepal, they'd have fitted about eight Sherpa in them!

We sat down on the floor of the tent and one of the porters came and introduced himself, saying he would be our waiter. That's right, a waiter on Kilimanjaro. He gave us each a bowl of hot water so we could wash our hands and faces.

Once we had finished washing, he collected the water bowl and said, 'Afternoon tea is ready.'

Ethan and I looked at each other, shocked. Luxury! Wow, this really was climbing in style.

The mess tent was set up with four chairs, and there was a huge array of drinks—coffee, tea, green tea, Milo, you name it—and heaps of food, including my old favourite, popcorn.

This camp was at 3000 metres, which isn't too high, so most people don't feel the altitude here. Ethan and I ate some afternoon tea, then had a snooze before dinner.

That night, the chef made a delicious curry, complete

with fresh meat and green vegetables, and for dessert there was canned fruit. Delicious.

Ethan and I played chess on my iPad, then settled into bed for our first night on Kilimanjaro together. We both slept really well. I think the travelling and then the 18-kilometre walk did the trick, and that night we could finally relax and just enjoy being on the mountain.

The next day's climb was a little steeper but it was only nine kilometres up to Shira camp. As we climbed, the views just got better and better, as we were out of the jungle and into the sub-alpine terrain.

The clouds rolled up the side of the mountain towards us, and would clear for a few minutes at a time, allowing us glimpses of the summit of Kilimanjaro. It felt like the mountain was teasing us. This brought an air of mystery to the place, as we knew the mountain was just there, towering over us, but we couldn't really get a good look at it.

The clouds rolled up the side of the mountain towards us, and would clear for a few minutes at a time, allowing us glimpses of the summit of Kilimanjaro. It felt like the mountain was teasing us.

Shira camp is at 3840 metres, but both of us were feeling really good. There were no headaches, and no sign of either of us losing our appetites. Dr Marc had prescribed us both Diamox, and we'd been taking it to help prevent altitude sickness. It looked like it was working.

We both slept well again, and woke up early for breakfast, ready for whatever the day was about to throw at us.

We had a 15-kilometre trek, which included walking

up to the Lava Tower, a volcanic rock tower that is a real Kilimanjaro icon. It stands at 4600 metres and the walk up to it is a great acclimatisation hike. From there, we were to head back down to the camp, which is at 3950 metres.

As we hiked, the climb got progressively harder throughout the day. Ethan and I were on our own and I found it a bit frustrating not knowing the landmarks as I do in the Himalaya. By the time I finally spotted the Lava Tower in the distance, Ethan was struggling a little. Even so, I knew we'd done the basics right. The atmosphere was getting thinner, so I'd made sure we both applied plenty of sunscreen throughout the day, and we'd been drinking as much water as we could and eating good snacks.

Quite a while later, we finally made it up to the tower, but we were exhausted. I can safely say we were both stoked to see that the team had set up a mess tent there and had lunch waiting for us. Ethan sat in a chair outside with his head in his hands. He was totally spent. It didn't take him long to perk up, though. A good plate of some nutritious food did the trick, and soon he was looking a lot better.

I decided I was going to make a cup of Milo, and film myself for a little video podcast, so I was describing to the camera exactly how I make it. 'The ratio is very important. Three scoops of Milo to one scoop of milk powder.'

'NO ONE CARES ABOUT YOUR MILK-POWDER RATIO, DAD!' Ethan shouted over my Milo monologue. Typical bloody teenager!

After lunch, Ethan was on fire. He was feeling really good, so he took off at quite a rapid pace. I had to keep reminding him to slow down as I was worried about his energy levels crashing. My advice fell on deaf ears, and he stayed about

200 metres ahead of me for the rest of the day. Ethan and I had found a good rhythm as a team, so every now and then he'd stop and wait for me.

A few hours later, we rolled into Barranco camp feeling tired but good. Up on Kilimanjaro, the sunsets were amazing. The clouds would slowly roll up the mountain's side in the most dramatic way. Almost as if someone was controlling their rise, the clouds would hit us just as the sun set in an array of colours. To start with, it would just be a thin, cold mist rolling in, which would be followed by full cloud as the temperature dropped.

Our stop the next night was to be at Karanga camp, which sits at 4200 metres. To get there was a six-kilometre trek, but it included climbing the Barranco wall. This involved a near-vertical climb straight up. Standing at the bottom of the wall, it looks very intimidating. We could see people already slowly snaking their way up it, so we watched them for a little while. Ethan and I talked about breaking the climb into tiny parts.

Salimu, the assistant guide, was with us. He fair motored his way up the wall, while Ethan and I did our best to follow him. The Barranco wall is a bit of a head game for anyone new to climbing. It's got a couple of parts that are pretty much vertical, which are about three or four metres high. If you fell from one of them, you'd hit a ledge. If you fell from the ledge, the drop would be a couple of hundred metres, I reckon.

At the top of the Barranco wall, the terrain flattens out a bit and there's an amazing view of the Western Breach of Kilimanjaro's crater wall. There was heaps of snow up there.

As we carried on towards Karanga camp, I got talking to

some other climbers who turned out to be from New York. I decided to wind them up a wee bit.

'Cool! I love New York. Hey, there is tonnes of snow on Kilimanjaro, eh?'

'I heard it was the most in twenty-five years,' the American guy said.

'You better make sure no one tells Donald Trump, as he doesn't believe in global warming, eh?' I said with a cheeky grin.

Thankfully, he laughed.

In the background, Ethan was rolling his eyes. 'Embarrassing, Dad,' he muttered.

That day, one of the young porters walked with us for a few hours. He didn't look like he was that much older than Ethan. He told us he was paid US$15 per day and hopefully a few more dollars from each client at the end of the trip. He said he was saving as much as he could so he could take an English course. If he spoke better English, he'd be able to be a guide and could earn more money for his family. The English course cost US$170. His life seemed like such a struggle, yet he was happy and smiled as we talked. Over the next few hours, we bumped into this porter a few times and Ethan really enjoyed chatting to him.

We arrived early into Karanga camp and settled in for the night. I was so impressed with the climb so far. The acclimatisation was going really well, and neither Ethan nor I had felt a single headache.

The next day was going to be huge. We were planning to trek to Barafu camp, which was at 4600 metres. We'd stay there until 10pm, when we would set off for the summit, which would be an all-night climb. The summit of

Kilimanjaro is 5895 metres high, so the climb from Barafu was a 1295-metre ascent. That is huge!

It takes a long time to get to the summit, and we had to set off at night in order to reach the top at dawn to see the sunrise. The guides would wake us at 10pm and we would have some tea and a little snack and be ready to leave at 11pm.

The trek to Barafu camp is like walking on Mars. It's a full alpine environment. There are no trees, just rocks and dust. Kilimanjaro is an extinct volcano so there are lots of different-coloured rocks that give it a slightly out-of-this-world feel.

We arrived at the high camp in time for afternoon tea and then tried to sleep. Unfortunately, out tent was right next to the porters' meeting point, so dozens of porters would gather there and talk loudly before setting off. It's situations like this that have taught me the importance of always having a good pair of earplugs with me, no matter where I am.

That night, we had dinner at the normal time and Mndeme came into the mess tent for a game of Guess Who?—this had become something of a ritual over the past few nights. It was so funny watching him play. He would ask questions like, 'Does your person have dark skin?' Not really a question we would normally ask back in New Zealand, as you would probably offend someone. Besides which, have you seen the different people in Guess Who? There are all sorts of skin shades, so we weren't quite sure whether Mndeme and us had the same idea of what 'dark skin' was!

Mndeme had been tracking all of our blood-oxygen saturation levels with a pulse oximeter. There was a rule that if your blood-oxygen saturation was below a certain level you were not allowed to even attempt the summit. I was really impressed by this.

When I was there in 2001, I'd suffered terrible altitude sickness. I don't even want to think what my levels were then. In those days, Kilimanjaro was the most dangerous mountain on the planet because so many people rushed up it, got altitude sickness and died. Things have clearly changed a lot since then—and for the better.

I said this to Mndeme. He replied, 'Yes, Mike, it was bad. Now we have better rules and things have changed. We also have better rescue teams with proper wheeled stretchers.'

He explained that part of the fee we'd paid to climb the mountain went towards any rescue services we might have needed. If one of us got sick, even at the summit, the guides would be able to get us down to the top camp and into one of the single-wheeled stretchers, and then we'd be whisked off the mountain.

With our oxygen levels checked and approved, Ethan and I headed for our tent to try to get some sleep before our 10pm climb time. Thankfully, all the porters had gone, so it was quiet. I don't know that it made much difference, though. We were both so excited that we barely slept.

CHAPTER 22

THE SUMMIT

At ten o'clock, Mndeme came over and woke Ethan and me up. He said he would be guiding us, which relieved a bit of my stress as he was super experienced. Ethan and I were both ready to go, but we had to wait around a bit for Prajod and Prasanna to get organised. I was used to this from my time guiding in Nepal, but it did worry me that it was very cold. Ethan and I stomped on the spot just to keep warm.

Finally, we were off, slowly moving upwards. The pace was incredibly slow, but I'm a firm believer that it doesn't matter how slow you go so long as you keep moving. It was very dark as there was no moon, but both Ethan and I had head torches so we could see where we were going.

Soon, we had left Prajod and Prasanna behind us and

were making good progress. It remained extremely cold. It was that type of bone-chilling cold that I'd only really felt on high-altitude mountains in the Himalaya, but then again we were at high altitude—this time in Africa. I had a down vest on, and I thought this would be warm enough, but my hands and feet were numb. I didn't want to tell Ethan as he was struggling with the cold too.

It was that type of bone-chilling cold that I'd only really felt on high-altitude mountains in the Himalaya.

He said his feet were numb, and I told him to keep wiggling his toes as much as he could. His hands were also worrying him. He was wearing ski gloves over another thin liner glove. I thought the combination would be fine, but it turned out that it wasn't warm enough. I rubbed his hands to get the circulation flowing again, then put his hands under my armpits to try to warm them up. I knew he must have been really cold as he didn't even mind!

As soon as his hands touched my skin, they felt like ice. I was very worried. But after a few minutes of having them in my armpits they warmed up and he was OK.

We set off again, knowing that we only had to struggle on until dawn, which was three or four hours away, and which would bring the warmth of the sun.

Another hour passed and Ethan's hands were cold again. This time, Mndeme pulled out a pair of high-quality mittens and gave them to Ethan. They were his emergency pair. With Ethan's hands sorted, it was time for a drink of water. We were stopping every 20 minutes or so to have some food, a handful of nuts or an energy bar, and some water. The water in our bottles had partly frozen, so I figured the temperature must have been about −15°C. Now that's cold, even by Himalayan standards!

Ethan sat down, had a small sip of water, then turned around and vomited.

I did a double-take. I thought I'd imagined it, as he had been going so well. He hadn't even mentioned he was feeling ill. Shock soon turned into concern, as I knew that vomiting was a serious sign of altitude sickness.

I turned to Mndeme and waved my hand across my throat, signalling to him that this was where we had to turn around. 'We need to go down, Mndeme. OK?'

'No, no, Mike. Just wait,' he said. 'Some people throw up and feel better and carry on.'

I wasn't convinced.

'No, Mike, trust me. If he is sick and has nausea then that's no good and we go down, OK? But if he is just tired, then we can handle just tired.'

I turned to Ethan, who was sitting on a rock, wiping the vomit from his chin. 'How are you feeling?' I asked him.

'No, Mike!' Mndeme said firmly. 'Wait until he has walked for ten minutes and then we ask.'

I must have looked very unhappy, as Mndeme leaned towards me and said quietly, 'You need to trust me. I've summited over 300 times, Mike. That's over 2000 clients and I've never lost anyone. Trust me.'

Even though it went against everything I'd been taught, something about Mndeme made me trust him. I took a deep breath and nodded. We got up and walked on.

Ten minutes later, I asked Ethan how he was feeling.

'Just tired, Dad. Just tired . . .'

I looked at Mndeme, who simply nodded.

Thankfully, Mndeme had been right.

With Ethan feeling better, we carried on up the mountain. The route seemed to go on forever. It was a real mind game to keep going at times. Some other climbers didn't win that particular game, and we watched them turn around and head back down without having made the summit. But we kept going—*polepole, polepole*—slowly moving up.

Eventually, we could see the ridge of the crater rim up in the distance. I knew that daybreak was coming, as the temperature started to rise ever so slightly. And we kept going and going.

At the exact moment the sun broke free and popped over the horizon, its rays hit our faces. They seemed exaggeratedly warm, as we'd been waiting for them for so long. With the warmth and colour that the sun brought, our spirits lifted.

I quietly said to myself, 'You're a good dad, Mike.' I don't think I'd ever let myself say those words out loud before.

We arrived at Stella Point on the crater rim. Ethan sat down, completely exhausted, his head in his hands. It was still another two hours to the summit.

A wave of emotion came over me. I felt pride welling up inside as I looked at my son on Kilimanjaro. The courage, the determination and the effort he had put in was amazing. I was so proud of him.

I started to think about being a good dad. Young boys need their dads, even if they can't see them all the time. A father figure in a young person's life is so important. I knew exactly what it was like to grow up without one and it was heart-breaking. I quietly said to myself, 'You're a good dad, Mike.' I don't think I'd ever let myself say those words out loud before, and instantly tears welled up in my eyes. I had to quickly think about something else, so that I didn't lose it altogether.

After a few sips of water and some snacks, we gathered ourselves together. It was time to make our way to the summit.

It wasn't long before we found ourselves walking on snow. All the climbers who had been here before us had compacted it into a track and it wasn't very steep, but there was still the risk of slipping and twisting an ankle to be mindful of.

I needn't have worried. Ever-organised Mndeme stopped and pulled two sets of crampons out of his rucksack—one for Ethan, and one for himself. Then off we went.

I have loads of experience on snow and ice so I thought I would be OK, but I soon regretted not having brought a pair of crampons. I was slipping and falling over every couple of minutes. If I wasn't careful it would be Ethan who would have to rescue me instead of the other way around.

Apart from my regular tumbles in the snow, we were doing well. The pace had slowed and Ethan was pushing hard, one foot in front of the other.

We got to a point where we could see the summit clearly just around the crater when Ethan stopped and slumped down into the snow, then vomited again! He threw up a lot, completely losing all his fluids. I was really concerned.

He had been dreaming about this adventure for a long time.

You have to have your own dreams and mountains in your life, I had told the kids.

Ethan and I had been planning for this very day for the past year.

To turn your adventures into reality, you have to build a strong plan.

I pulled Ethan to his feet, put my arm around him and said, 'I'm so proud of you, Ethan. I really am. You have done so well. This can be our summit—OK?'

I'll never forget what he said to me than for as long as I live. There was a long pause as he caught his breath, then he said, 'No, Dad, I'm never, never giving up.'

I dried the tears from my eyes and together we climbed the last few metres to the summit of Kilimanjaro together, father and son.

▲

You never, never give up on your dreams in life.

Every single one of us has a beautiful rocking chair waiting for us at the end of our life. It might be a short time away or a long time away, but all of us will be sitting in that rocking chair wishing for just a little more time. Kids at seven years old and teenagers spell love the same way: T-I-M-E. And time is precious, so go out and make the most of that time and . . .

Conquer your mountains.

Mike Allsop
Adventurer, airline pilot, speaker and,
most importantly, very, very proud dad

POSTSCRIPT

Ethan and I managed to play the world's highest board game, getting in two rounds of Guess Who? on the summit of Kilimanjaro. Ethan won both times. Guinness World Records are currently considering the record.

Ethan raised over $1200 for the Auckland City Mission. He has just gone solo in a small plane and is working towards being a pilot one day.

I'll be guiding my first group up Kilimanjaro in 2019.

Wendy is planning an adventure to Scotland to explore castles and history.

Maya is playing representative football and asking Dad when she can guide an Everest base camp adventure with him.

Dylan is still dreaming up ideas for his 14-year-old adventure with Dad. Watch this space.